M000279472

ACTING CLASS

Take A Seat

MILTON KATSELAS

ACTING
CLASS

Take A Seat

ISBN-10: 1-59777-592-4
ISBN-13: 978-1-59777-592-2
Library of Congress Cataloging-In-Publication Data Available

Book Design by: Sonia Fiore
Cover Design by: Mark Porro

Printed in the United States of America

Phoenix Books, Inc.
9465 Wilshire Boulevard, Suite 840
Beverly Hills, CA 90212

10 9 8 7 6 5 4 3 2 1

This book is dedicated to all the actors
I've met, and those I've yet to meet....
and for Mary and Tasso.

Special thanks to Allen Barton for
his support and dedicated work
in editing this book.

Table of Contents

Acting

Attitude

Administration

Preface

As I sit to write this preface, I think back to the first version of this book, which has been used in my classes for years. It has existed for over three decades in the form sitting before me on my desk, a three-ring binder with a soft leather cover. I liked this format because it had a workman-like feel, which allowed me to make revisions, additions, and to riff on new thoughts about acting and actors as they've occurred to me over time. It is for this reason that until now I never published the book—it allowed me room to move, to change, to respond, to meditate on my own lessons learned as a director and teacher, and in turn to pass that illumination on to students.

Actors who have come to my school, The Beverly Hills Playhouse, have received this book at the beginning of their journey with me. It's written in a very direct style, often using transcribed critiques with real students to illustrate concepts. Most of the narrative articles were written based on talks I have given, many improvised on the spot, to groups of living, breathing actors sitting in front of me—often full of hope, frustration, desire, fear, sadness, joy—both sulking and enthusiastic, or more likely, all these colors all at once, varying face by face as I look upon them.

Up until now, the best way for actors to understand my approach is to sit in one of my classes, feel the energy of the room, do a scene, get a critique—and through that experience see if this helps them understand and change and improve. This book is an effort to bring that experience alive to any reader, actor or non-actor alike, Los Angeles-based, New York-based, or anywhere in the world.

The class is headquartered on Robertson Boulevard in Beverly Hills—as you walk down a shaded courtyard toward the theatre, you'll notice a large tree stretching above you to the sky between buildings. You see that students enjoy relaxing in the courtyard, and on breaks during class it is full of actors talking energetically about their next scene, or the play they're doing, or the film they're shooting, or what they're doing to move their career forward. Notice the bust of Tennessee Williams—the great American writer I admire, and had the good fortune to work with as a director. He's always looking at the courtyard with a bemused expression that cracks me up and reminds me of his unique humor—humor that is often missed by actors performing his work. The entrance door is black, and above it the word "Theatre" is handwritten in white paint from when this building was first built in the 1930s.

A small hallway leads to the theatre space, where the seats are upholstered in a burgundy fabric, arranged in a gentle arc before the elevated black stage. The class feels enthusiastic, and I like the energy of all those students—it is infectious, and performing for a full house puts a little pressure on the actors performing tonight—I want them to feel supported, safe even, but also challenged.

As I enter, the students like to applaud, but frankly I'm not into all that stuff, I don't really believe it. But it helps mark the beginning of class and I'm not one to squelch enthusiasm, even if it's somewhat made up. I can tell who's making it up and who's genuine as I cross to sit in my chair. The lights dim, the noise subsides, the stage manager announces the first scene to be performed. The curtain opens. So go on, take a seat.

Dare To Be An Artist

Genius is not a possession of the limited few,
but exists to some degree in everyone.
—Robert Henri, American painter and author

MILTON: Actually, hold on a second. Before you begin the scene...we have some new people here tonight, and I wanted to greet them with a little talk. *(To actors on stage:)* Sorry—good training for film. You're all ready to shoot the big scene and then just before they call "action!" something comes up.... The lights aren't right, a costume is being questioned, and you have to wait. Or the director gets a call from his ex-wife or something. I personally would not take that call.

Laughter from class.

So, I was thinking today about all of you. What led you here, to Los Angeles, to this class. I think you come with a dream. Sometimes these dreams are real, or they are fancies, glimmers of thought, a flickering image of something desired. I want the class to help focus, define, and realize these dreams—to lead each of you to your own personal way, your own personal definition and expression. To be an artist is the most important contribution a human being can make. Don't ever minimize the genius that lies within you. Every effort must be made to free the creative spirit in you, and so make a life and an artist who is relevant.

So what is an acting class about, anyway? For me, the study of acting is really the study of life. This seemingly obvious truth can get hidden by the fact that acting

1

study has aspects of technical work and exercise work, and this can sometimes, mistakenly in my opinion, make a class too academic. But Stella Adler corroborated something I had been doing for 15 years as a teacher when she told me, "I'm not teaching acting, darling. I'm teaching actors to be people." It is the fusing of your skill as an artist and your knowledge of life as a person that will help you truly communicate through your work.

Remember that all you express as an artist comes from you. Cary Grant once spoke here in class, and said in his delicious accent, "All you have is you, you know." Then the great director Martin Ritt came, and in his gruff voice said, "All you've got to mine is the gold within yourself." Here were two quite opposite artists, both emphasizing the same point: It's about you. Your life, your experiences, your memories, your body are going to affect the character you're playing—and you need to light up those elements to provide that personal touch. Dare to make it *your* personal Hamlet, your unique Romeo, your own Cyrano—and not just for these classic roles, but for the new, original roles that are coming your way, waiting for you to mark them with your personal branding iron.

I don't mean to scare away any of the new students here tonight, but part of my job as a teacher is to make clear that middle-class thinking and habits inhibit creativity. The artist is afraid to express himself from fear of being criticized or condemned. Starting as a child, the words *don't, watch out, don't do that, be quiet, be careful, be still* —these and countless other expressions ruled the child's life and influenced his future. I've met innumerable actors in whom I can see a certain risky, wild creativity wanting to come out—but it's been suppressed. Modesty and humility tend to rule the day. You know the derivation of *humility*, or *humble*? Lowly. Submissive. The ground. The dirt. These are not qualities very useful to an actor. Well, I can think of one or two who could use a bit of it....

A ripple of laughter from the class.

But as much as I'm trying to unleash this highly expressive, personal artist, I'm also trying to unleash the *mensch* within all actors—you all know from *mensch?* Show of hands? A couple people. I thought we had more people of the Jewish persuasion in class. *Mensch* is Yiddish for being a full person, a human being who cares, who has a heart, who can communicate easily, and be easily communicated to. Theatre and film work are group activities, so the ability to work well within a group dynamic is vital to the long-term prospects of your careers. My aim is twofold: a highly creative individual actor who also can flourish and contribute to the growth of a strong group.

Dare to say that you have real genius in you. Dare to believe that in your personal thoughts and feelings lives a real artist worthy of self-expression and the world's appreciation. Dare to know that you are an artist capable of creating and revealing some aspect of life. Dare to learn, explore, participate and feel the joy of this meaningful journey. You all getting me?

CLASS: Yes!

MILTON: Good. Make sure you say hi to the new people— make them feel at home. Okay. *(Turns to actors on stage:)* So very nice of you to wait to do the scene. You're pros, right? Alright. Let's rock and roll.

My Approach

Acting, Attitude, and Administration—these are the broad areas of my teaching. Acting is of course the craft, the technique, the process by which you create your work. By Attitude I mean the viewpoint and feeling of the artist towards his life, towards himself and what he creates, towards his fellow artists and all of the people in his life. Administration—this is the area where the actor, through specific choices and specific actions that are then carried out, puts this talent and attitude effectively into the world, and so moves his or her career forward. I believe that in order to create a complete actor, a real artist who can function well for the long haul in this business, each of these three areas, inextricably linked to one other, must be cooking. A long-term career is a constant dance between the three. Let me dive in a bit further on each:

ACTING

When I was a young boy, my father said to me, "Know thyself." It sounds even better in Greek, and more imposing when you have a guy like my father standing over you as you hear it. I think acting affords you the best opportunity to know yourself. Acting is a noble and respected field of the arts, and in my opinion the most personal. It gives you the opportunity to understand your fellow man through the depiction and experience of living even a fraction of his life. There are essentially two ways actors go about this journey—two different intentions: One is that of the poser, the indicator, the phony, and the other is that of the honest actor who tries in his or her own way to live the experience of the

5

character. My approach is geared to the latter, toward helping that honest actor develop a very personal experience.

There are many choices an actor can make to create a very personal connection, including using his imagination. But I'm really interested in the Greek actor in ancient times about whom I read; he had to play a scene, and this actor brought an urn to the amphitheatre and placed it on the altar onstage—an urn filled with the ashes of his own son who had died. In an unflinching way, he brought to his acting one of the most personal and painful objects in his life, to help fire him up as an actor. That certainly turns me on as a teacher, that quest for a personal connection to the role.

It's easy to look at Marlon Brando's work and identify it as acting I'm interested in—I truly believe his work is a high mark in the field of acting—always human, personal, always intelligent, and often filled with unexpected humor.

The unexpected. I like that in an actor. I generally prefer sports to acting, because in sports you just never know what is really going to happen. In any sport, no matter the odds, there is always the possibility of an upset, the last second shot, the hail-Mary pass, a wild play that leads to the unexpected failure of the better team, the underdog comes out ahead—these possibilities keep me glued to a good game. A fine basketball player will discover the open man at the last second—that split-second discovery is key to the excitement. So part of my approach is to give the actor tools for creating an acting experience filled with discovery, spontaneity, surprise, and freshness.

If I were to bottom-line it, I would say that I want the acting to be real. I want its foundation at the very least to represent life as we know it. When an actor is doing something on stage, I want him really to be doing it, or at least a damned good likeness of it. If an actor is on the telephone, I want to feel that the particular character to whom he's talking is on the other end. *Specifically.* If he's playing a butcher, he should know how to carve the meat so that any butcher in the audience believes him. If the characters are in love, I want to feel the intense affinity and feverishness that love can inspire. And not the cornball fake swooning stuff—I mean the real deal, so that I believe they're really in love. Shakespeare said love is a disease, and I want to see that—if it's the kind of love that the Bard is talking about, where obsession rules, let's experience it—go for it.

But simple reality isn't always enough. It's the foundation—and without it you're going to have real problems most of the time. But moving past a baseline reality, we come to the imagination of the actor, an expressiveness, an intelligence, the unexpected moment, the use of irony and humor to deal with difficult situations. Definitely humor, so that even those naturalistic coffee-shop scenes are elevated to a new level—as in *When Harry Met Sally.* Or the way Cary Grant cracked me up—even in the tense Hitchcock dramas, he maintained that charm and irony. Look, I admire Lucille Ball and what she did on that television show. It was hilarious, madcap, but had at the root of it a reality, the reality of her relationship with Desi Arnaz. Maybe there are not a lot of people who would put Marlon Brando and Lucille Ball in the same sentence, but both of them interest me and I like both of their work. So I'm not just about *serious acting.* I love to entertain, and be entertained. I've assigned some of my most talented and serious students to do some pretty madcap stuff in class.

But if you held my feet over the fire and insisted I succinctly describe my approach to acting, I'd say I come at it like the director I am. I ask all sorts of questions. What's the story? What do people do when dealing with events like these? How do they respond? What's their behavior? I want a real-person, real-place, real-behavior approach to the work, not a sketch, not a skit, not a glib attempt—I want the real deal. And then of course, imagination, humor, surprises, irony, intelligence—the whole enchilada.

So how do I get actors to do this kind of work? I'm sure the question goes around the acting community—what kind of teacher is he? Is he a Meisner guy, a Strasbergian, an Adlerite, a Hagenist...? I've been fortunate enough to work with and closely observe all those very talented teachers, as well as apprenticing as a young director with Josh Logan and Elia Kazan. I've observed the masters, and I've worked with actors myself for almost half a century. Through all that, I've developed my own way of teaching, but it derives a lot from my career as a director. As a director I frankly don't care how the actor does it. I have limited time, limited money, the sun is going down, we're losing our light, and we have to shoot, we have to get film in the can. If I discover that an actor does a fabulous job every time he jumps rope before a scene, then I'm buying that guy a rope every time. I don't care what thoughts he has in his trailer, what exercises he is doing or not doing in his dressing room. The star working opposite that guy may have her own way of working, quite different from the other actor, and I need to understand that and communicate to her differently—she doesn't jump rope and buying her a rope will do nothing for her. That's directing. My job is to find out how to communicate to this actor in front of me, discover the language that will best help each individual understand and believe in my vision of the story.

In teaching, it's still very individual. I look at the particular actor in front of me, and try to deduce what he or she needs, try to find the language and images that will lead them to understand acting better. It's very individual. I have certain exercises you will read about, and different actors may need to work with them in different ways. But across the board, I would say I look at this individual actor, and when working on a script—whether a play or film—I try to get them to understand *the story*. What events are associated with this story, what is the specific nature of this character, what happened to them before this scene, what is the behavior associated with the scene, and how can this particular actor, with all his or her uniqueness, bring it all to life in an organic, personal, human way? *What would a real person do in this given circumstance?* Those are the things I emphasize to the actor. It's simple. It's hard sometimes to see the simplicity in acting, and the actor often wants to make it complex, which then makes acting more difficult. So I try to keep it simple, and clear.

ATTITUDE

I've found over the years that attitude monitors talent, just as the aperture on a camera lens monitors light. A small aperture—marked by attitudes like hostility, a chip on the shoulder, the monotonous whining sound of a victim, a spoiled "I don't wanna work" viewpoint—allows very little of the light, namely, your talent, to come through. And so a negative attitude can very much affect your performances, your auditions, your relations with the people important to moving your acting career forward. But open up that lens with a good attitude—enthusiastic, willing to learn, cooperative, charming, full of self-esteem—this will affect every moment of your life, and let more of your acting talent come through. This is why you observe the phenomenon that actors who may not be the most talented in the world, but who have a great attitude, often can have very rewarding careers, while those with the most talent, but with a bad attitude, can become embittered and seemingly stuck.

There are, of course, innumerable reasons why any person can have a negative attitude of one kind or another. In instances where I can spot it, I will try as best I can to help the actor deal with the attitude, get them to realize they can change it for the better. I try to listen, get their point of view, and then use charm, humor, toughness, whatever is needed to help them make that change. But I can't always be there to help in this way, and my job is to train actors to do it for themselves—the acting work, the attitude, everything. My real interest is in persuading my students not to use their psychological problems as an excuse for not working at the top of their game. I learned this from the great director Josh Logan when I worked for him. He described to me an experience he had with Janet Blair, who was getting ready to star in the road company of *South Pacific,* in the role that Mary Martin had originated on Broadway. Martin was the be-all and end-all of musical comedy performers, and Janet was intimidated by her, and it was affecting her ability to bring the role to life. Josh told me how he went to her room and simply spoke to her about her talent, asked about her life, her family. He said she was soundly changed by the conversation, felt more confident, and that this became evident in her performance. And that was when I realized that properly assessing and dealing with the attitude of the actor was an important aspect of being a director. That hadn't been covered in university.

A good attitude is really about enthusiasm, which at its Greek roots means "energy from the Gods." Actors can often be a notoriously moody bunch, full of insecurities, hostility, and 31 other dubious flavors of negativity, and I for one want to change that whenever I see it. I'm looking to rehabilitate that energy of the gods. An actor with a good attitude has the ability to handle his fellows, solve problems, using a positive manner to make every set and stage they're on a better place to be for everyone. I feel attitude is a crucial component in the actor's overall health and potential for success—many actors have been hired and re-hired simply because it's a pleasure to have them around for the strenuous and lengthy hours of work that are demanded by theatre and film projects.

ADMINISTRATION

An actor in tune with his administration is an effective, proactive artist who makes smart choices to enhance his career and its potential for development, as well as his very life, *and sees to it that these choices are carried out.* I believe the actor is the true manager, the true administrator of his or her career. Skilled and dedicated agents and managers can help along the way for sure, but my observation is that too many actors take a back seat when driving their own car. So once I have an actor on my hands who I believe does consistently good work, and whose attitude is aligned with that talent, my next question is: What choices are you making about your career, and are these choices moving it forward? Are you taking the actions you need to put your talent and your good attitude into the world? Do you write letters to directors whom you admire, congratulating them on their latest project, or keeping-in-touch notes to people you've auditioned for or worked with in the past? Are you up to date on the tools for promoting yourself on the Internet? As I've written in my book *Dreams Into Action,* administration can also include having a clean, bright happy place to live, a real desk of your own where you can work, and handling your finances so you aren't stressed by that issue. It includes the actions you take in the real world to keep your attitude in check—if you know a morning workout puts you in a better frame of mind for the day ahead, then that is part of your administration. "Admin," as it is referred to by my students, includes the scheduling of your busy life to ensure you make your rehearsals on time, getting enough sleep, doing well at your day jobs. It's knowing about fashion, looking good, not using drugs and alcohol, going to art galleries, deepening your knowledge as an artist and a person. All of these choices are just about being smart, doing the right thing for your life and your career. More artists have screwed themselves up by lack of administration than by lack of talent. Unlike composers, writers and painters, the actor cannot be discovered after he dies. So I want you all to be working actors now, and administration plays a key role.

So we have these three areas of work—Acting, Attitude and Administration. I meet up against them in class every day. Over there is an actor full of hostility, a chip on his shoulder the size of Colorado, but I'll try to charm him, befriend him, get him to smile, and just talk to him about the acting. For him, I feel the answer is that personal connection, and the craft—getting detailed and real with the work itself. Next to that guy is a young actress whose talent is unbelievable, but she's withdrawn and insecure, and if she could just lighten up and be more charming and believe in herself a bit more, the talent would explode—and with her I do talk about that attitude issue. And behind her is the dark horse, the underdog, the one you would never think could be successful, but he quietly writes a great letter to a known director, gets a meeting from that, and lands a part—he passes all the other students on the freeway from administration alone. That's how I did it.

But I don't want you to think the class itself is 33.3% Acting, 33.3% Attitude, and 33.3% Administration. The foremost emphasis is *acting*—the development of the craft, the technique, the ability and creativity of the actor. I speak of attitude and administration only to facilitate and enhance the power of a skilled actor to do his or her work and get it out there into the world. All the attitude and administration in the world will be for naught if we don't have actors who know what they are doing. In the end, the craft, the work—that's what's most important.

All You Can Be

Don't minimize your acting because of your life. Please try not to justify that you can't do something in your acting because of what you can't do in your life. *Don't use your psychology as an excuse for not being able to execute something in your art.* Instead, use acting to do that which you can't do in your mundane life. So, in a sense, to hell with psychology. Go for the art. Get interested in art, and who knows—maybe the psychology will improve. In your art you can bound over and beyond anything that you believe is limiting you.

Art is not just about you, but about the *possibilities* of you. It's an odd part of my teaching, but sometimes when a student in a critique offers up some personal fear or insecurity as a reason the role was difficult, here's my answer: "No one cares. Not a single person. No one in this room. No one in any other room." It sounds a bit harsh, but, unfortunately, it's true. No one cares about how your problems limit your art or your life. The casting director doesn't care, the critic doesn't care. In the end, the director doesn't care. They all want the result, the answer. We'll only care if you take a problem, like your fear or insecurity, and turn it into Joan of Arc's courage. We care about how you *surmount* that problem. It's possible that some actor, less talented than you, but without the excuse of having this particular problem, will snatch the part right from under you, and pass you on the freeway. I don't want that. I want you doing the passing.

This is where I am, this is who I am, therefore, this is all I can give. No. Too limited. Instead: *This is what I have in my fantasy, this is what I have in my imagination, this is what I can give. Not what I think I am, but what I dream I can be. What I truly want to be. I live in my art through my passion, my fantasy, not my mundane reality.* The gossip is that Frank Lloyd Wright was at times petty. But he wasn't petty when he sat at a drawing table. Are you going to study his rumored pettiness or are you going to study his drawings, his buildings? An inflammatory pop biography portrays Picasso as an egomaniacal monster. Just look at the humanity in the body of his work. His painting, his sculpture, his pottery were all sublime. Alec Guinness lived a quiet, conservative English country life. Put him on stage in a dress and he was wildly imaginative. So they tell you Martin Luther King is alleged to have done this or done that; who cares? I don't care if it was true; I don't care if it's untrue. What I care about is that he was one of the greatest speakers and spiritual leaders of all time. One of the greatest that has ever graced our planet. It was his *dream* that he followed, not the mundane reality of the world around him, which he was actually seeking to change.

An actor in my classes once said to me, "I've always been the second banana." As we talked, he spoke to me about having been the gofer for Marvin Gaye: "Go for coffee, go for sandwiches." I replied, "Jesus, you're a powerful, sexy man. You're not a gofer anymore." Something seemed to shift within him. Two weeks later, we played basketball together and he played very differently: Tough, in a new winning way. Immediately his work as an actor took an enormous leap. He ended up becoming a wonderful talent, quite successful in films and television, and later even developed into quite a powerful teacher in his own right. Second banana, see ya later.

As a teacher, I look at everyone not as they are, but rather in terms of what they're capable of being. I don't ever see before me some struggling, self-centered actor wrestling with his or her career or day-to-day problems. I just don't. I see artists. Powerful, influential artists. And I will only relate to you on that level, the level to which you should be striving to reach. I'm aiming towards and only interested in who you can be and what you can create as an artist.

Study: Why and How?

MILTON: Before we take a break here, I thought I'd cover something that was on my mind today. (*To actors on the stage:*) Why don't you guys sit down—good job, excellent. Give them a hand, will you?

Class applauds.

One of the big challenges in teaching actors to improve their craft—or in my case to improve Acting, Attitude and Administration.... You guys look blank. You heard of those three topics, right? Or is it news to you? It's kind of the basis of my approach....

Nervous laughter.

That was a very nervous laugh. Commitment. That's the challenge in teaching. To get the actor to commit. We live in a push-button, remote-control society, where people's attention spans do nothing but decrease year after year, where unrelenting media delivery hurls information at you from every direction 24 hours a day. A simple, quiet room is practically unheard of.

This cacophony of bells and whistles and alarms and cell phone rings and laptops powering up and powering down and skin glowing blue from the light of some computer display inches from your face, and you disappear into the glow, life itself becomes secondary....

Class laughter.

...All this shit has increased exponentially in the last ten years, that's why I start some classes with the ironic comment, "Please make sure your cell phones are on—thanks." Ah, the irony of it all. But in this kind of environment, it is increasingly difficult to focus, to put your nose to the grindstone, and work at your craft in a concentrated way. This computer jazz can affect you if you're not careful, you can become this inert sponge—sitting for hours, "surfing," vacuous, soaking up millions of unrelated pieces of information, images, videos—jumbled and jangled and meaningless. Getting all into "data," rather than your imaginations. Anyway, I digress. The point is there isn't a decent tradesperson or doctor or lawyer or teacher or musician or dancer or you-name-it who hasn't earned his or her status through years of training, work and experience. Acting is no different.

Work ethic is a huge part of developing a good actor. In this class I want you to be safe—but challenged. You should feel safe, and yet challenged enough to risk. This is your gym. So break a sweat. I want you to work hard, and with this challenge and some enthusiasm on your part, there will be no such thing as failure. When you learn, there is no failure.

I see many of you radiating a state of continuous, subtle panic about the issue of *getting work*—you're spun in ten different directions at once by the advice of friends, family, agents, managers...I don't like the smell or look of this panic. It's not helpful. The allure of the almighty dollar can distort your viewpoint about training. You might sometimes hear the question: *Why on earth should you keep studying?* The subtext of that question is a sort of dubious, negative one. Listen—musicians graduating from Juilliard still have to practice every day to stay sharp, and often have teachers to guide the way even as they are having successful careers. I know you and everyone around you want you to be successful, and I want that too. But mainly I'm interested in your being a really good actor. Musicians can practice alone. The actor needs a group in order to stay focused and improve. Class provides you that group.

There is a common misconception that actors who are studying in an acting class cannot act, or "have not made it yet." Some people even feel that someone in an acting class is not truly professional. The attitude exists that what's really important is networking, Hollywood parties, all that jazz. But I once had a student who was having dinner with Oliver Stone, and left the dinner early to get to class. You'd think this was crazy, but you know what? Stone respected that. Not weeks later, Stone visited the class and told me he respected the fact that instead of bowing meekly before social convention and a networking homerun—*dinner with Oliver Stone!*—this actor took his leave to get some training that night.

Now, someone last week spoke to me outside because he was concerned about another actor here, whether she was "at the right level." You know, would this other student, a newer person, bring the class down, that kind of thing. Early in my career, a very good actor called me to inquire about joining my class—he asked slightly skeptically, "Who's in the class?" I wasn't polite in response—I told him all he needed to know is that I was teaching it, and if the students were good enough for me, then they were good enough for him. Then I hung up. He started the class. I personally like different talent and experience levels intermingling. And I vote for the underdog. Every group you will ever be involved with, be it film, television, or theatre, has within it all the different strata of talent, technique, and personalities that one finds in any acting class. So I think a class should be a microcosm of what the actor will face in all of his professional life.

The bottom line of all this is I want you guys fervent. I want a class of fervent, feverish, boiling-hot actors. Harold Clurman wrote a book, which probably very few of you have read, and you should read it; it's about The Group Theatre in the 1930s and he called it *The Fervent Years*. Over my time as a teacher, I have given various talks about, "Get it together, get your enthusiasm and your energy up." But what I'm saying is really beyond that. This is beyond "Get your energy up for the class." This is about a passion that burns within you, that brings you to your rehearsal, that keeps you up at night about your work as an actor. And I realize this is not the kind of talk that should be given at this time in Hollywood. I know that. Your agents are not propelling you with this kind of talk. Your friends and cohorts are not sitting around talking like this. You're not investing this kind of fervency in your communication with your fellows and trying to instill it more and more in yourself and in your work. You have some of it. Don't think I don't see it. But I wonder what percent of you would qualify on the level that I am talking about. And how would that affect your life, your work, your career, your family, your pocketbook, and more than all of that—your sense of well-being? There is no life without fire—spiritual and artistic fire. This is the very fuel of our lives. The fire I speak of has to do with passion and exuberance. When you feel strongly, you will create an underlying heat that fuels your journey.

So you have to have the passion within that propels you to burn a barn, you have to be on fire. And politeness is not the answer. And likeability is not the answer. That doesn't mean you've got to be a shit, it doesn't mean that. But it also doesn't mean that you qualify by being likeable and being nice. You have a job to do, you have a fervent passion, and you go and do it. In other decades there were these causes that artists would get behind— communism, World War II, anti-communism, civil rights, Vietnam, gay rights, Greenpeace, what have you—and maybe the current society is such you don't feel there is that *cause* that moves you. So that means without a cause, the cause has to be the art of it, the art within you. The fervency about that and about what you want to do and what you want to say, no matter whether you have a cause to back it or not. But the fact is that George Clooney—he makes movies dealing with shit he cares about. Vanessa Redgrave. Susan Sarandon. Sean Penn. Spike Lee—you think that guy doesn't have fervor? And you can love him or hate him, but Michael Moore does that in the documentary world. He's burning barns.

My hope is that a good class inspires this fervor within you. And no doubt, you will meet obstacles—but remember, you have a dream, and you are taking practical steps toward the fulfillment of that dream. I believe in you. You must believe in you. And listen, man, it's supposed to be fun, supposed to be a joy to study. On a less high-falutin' note, it was the great teacher Herbert Berghoff who said about class, "Better here than bowling."

Class laughter.

Okay, let's take a break....

My Goals as a Teacher

GOAL

• An acting profession of responsible, effective artists who contribute to the revitalization of our society through their creative work in theatre and film.

PURPOSE

• To develop the actor's talent to the fullest, and to encourage the actor to be positive and effective in life and art.

• To develop actors, directors, and writers who produce theatre and film projects that excite, entertain, and have strong aesthetic values.

PRODUCT

Artists who:

• Have a strong desire for excellence and achievement.

• Have the intention to succeed against all odds; real leaders with integrity and ethics.

• Are good group workers, with upbeat dispositions; cheery and of high morale.

• Are always seeking to be better, and exploring the potentials of their talent.

• Are able to keep consistently healthy in body and mind.

• Have the ability to create quality communications that produce the desired emotional results, and bring to the audience understanding.

Acting

The Checklist

Acting is ephemeral, difficult to nail down, different for every actor, and often different for the same actor from role to role. But there are techniques that can resolve problems, and lead you to creative solutions. By technique, I mean anything that helps you fulfill the art of acting. In the simplest sense, technique is all that you do to create a work of art. If an actor runs around the block before a scene to help trigger an emotion, that's technique. If a painter ritualistically rearranges his studio before each session, that's technique. If a writer uses the sense memory of childhood aromas to launch into a new chapter, that's technique. If a director takes responsible control of his life so that creative time can be better managed, that's technique. From the smallest, seemingly insignificant action you do while rehearsing, to the most complicated exercise or character study, all is technique.

In all work on technique, I believe there are two components: **Work on a Role,** and **Work on Oneself.** For an actor, these two are completely entwined: work on oneself, which can include work on body, voice, and exercises or improvisations to open up emotionally. Then work on a role, the specifics of that character in the story, which can affect work on oneself and vice versa. Many an actor has learned a lot about himself and life through the work on a specific role, and I might add that, whether they know it or not, this is part of the reason they are drawn to acting as a profession. The actor is both the creator and the created. In other performing arts such as music, the artist plays an instrument, but the actor is both the player and the instrument. Under pressure of the immediacy of a performance, the actor has nothing else but himself.

Art has to do with the delivery of a strong communication. This communication for an actor goes first to his partner, and then to the audience. This impact on the acting partner and then the audience is more important than getting caught up in some special, elitist technique. Communication first, technique second. Use technique, don't let it use you. Technique is a means to an end, not an end in itself.

What follows here is referred to by the students in class as "The Checklist." It has evolved over my years of teaching as a series of tools any actor can use to help approach their work on a scene. A very successful actress who has been a student of mine for a long time insists she uses this checklist on every gig she gets. It is not strictly necessary to dwell upon the entire checklist every time you work—any one of the tools may be the one that unlocks a scene for you.

1. The Event
2. Evaluation
3. Behavior
4. Physical/Emotional State
5. What Happened Before the Scene?
6. Creative Hiding
7. Be a Person
8. Inner and Outer Life: The "Cover"
9. Who's the Author?
10. Improvisation
11. Humor
12. Trust

1. THE EVENT

By "event" I mean what is happening in a scene. What is taking place? My favorite question when directing: *"What's going on?"* Is it a wedding, as in the opening of *The Godfather?* The wedding is the main event, the primary reason the family has gathered. The other strong event is the people approaching the Godfather to congratulate him or, more importantly, to ask him for favors.

When you understand the event—*what is going on here?* —you can then connect that answer to your own life, the experiences that you may have had that relate in some way to the event in this story, and so in that way understand the story better.

In thinking about the event, don't tie yourself in knots. It's not academic. You needn't write an essay. Just try to answer the simple question, "What's going on?" Many times I ask this question and immediately can sense the actor going astray: "Well, it's a piece about redemption." Wrong. It may very well be a piece about redemption, but *what's going on?* It might take a few times of my asking to get to something like, "I'm packing my stuff to move out on this relationship." Oh! Now *that* I can play. I understand that. That's an event. Everyone has had a breakup scene or two in their life. So ask yourself: What did I do? How did I behave? How did I respond? An understanding of the event and relating it to something personal from your life, a behavior or emotion you can draw upon, should set you on a course of acting that is specific, real and personal.

You must look carefully and study the facts of a scene in order to determine the actual event. Sometimes in acting, as in life, there is an apparent event and then an actual event. In the rape scene in *A Streetcar Named Desire*, the apparent event is Stanley coming home to celebrate the birth of his child, but the actual event is Stanley's seduction of Blanche, eventually raping her. Some other examples:

> **Apparent event:** A funeral of a loved one, with appropriate black clothes and weeping around the casket. **Actual event:** Everyone is wondering who will get the money? Who's in the will? Who's crying the most to show they deserve the inheritance the most?

> **Apparent event:** In class, an actor volunteers to help a beautiful actress with her career administration or her scene work, full of creative ideas to improve her journey in class. **Actual event:** The actor, fancying the actress, wants to do anything to ingratiate himself—the actual event is fueled by romantic desire.

> **Apparent event:** An uncle tries very hard to support his niece, and guide her in her romantic experience with a boy to whom she's attracted. **Actual event:** The uncle has his own attraction to her, against the morals of society, and is secretly trying to break up the

young couple for his own purposes. (This particular example is of course from Arthur Miller's *A View From the Bridge.)*

In the play, *The Girl on the Via Flaminia,* an American soldier is fixed up with a young Italian girl who he brings to live with him as his mistress. They meet for the first time in a room of an Italian *pensione.* The event is clear, except for an important detail: the girl is a virgin. Her innocence adds a special circumstance to the event for both the actress and the actor playing the scene. This scene is played differently by both because she is a virgin. The event is different, her behavior is different, and the boy's reactions toward her are different. It is not stated in the play that she is a virgin, but if you examine the story closely—*what's actually going on here?* It seems to me an Italian family hiding their sixteen or seventeen-year-old daughter from the Germans, and now from the American GIs, would have protected her and not let her out of their sight. Now the war is over, she's about twenty, and still a virgin. In this scene, an actor must look carefully to pull this important but unstated fact, which strongly affects the actual event.

Again, once the actors nail down the event, they can then look into their own personal experience to better understand the event, and how specifically to play it. They can say, "Oh, I remember the first time I had sex, what the scene was like, how nervous I was, how I behaved." Because it was so long ago, some actors may have forgotten that at one time they actually were virgins. So check it out, it'll come back to you! This connection of the events of a play or film to one's own experience is vital. It makes the events personal to *you—* specific, real, and alive.

I recall doing a project once at the Actors' Studio in New York. The scene was an Armistice celebration party at the end of World War I, a scene from Bud Schulberg's *The Disenchanted*. Rather than a stilted stage party, we created a fluid, free-flowing, very lively party. The action continued while the principals, isolated by follow spotlights, carried on their dialogue, which was an innovative solution to a party scene on stage. The understanding and full use of the event—the exuberant party—freed us to discover this solution. *The Disenchanted* is about the F. Scott Fitzgeralds. One could say Zelda and Scott's life together in the '20s was a party. So here they are meeting for the first time, symbolically, at a violent, erotic, romantic party. We really nailed this event, the celebration of the end of World War I, which defined for the actors the wild life of their characters. This furious activity in our scene was carried out fully, enhancing the two lead actors' specific participation in the event. They could flirt with other partygoers in the middle of the scene, or be dragged off into the fray by someone who wanted to dance. The actors playing Zelda and Scott were able to feel the presence of this mad crowd surrounding them as they danced in their midst, to feel the seductive energy of this volatile time, which was a foreshadowing of their chaotic life to come. The event is a very strong tool, helping you unlock the scene—so look carefully, get the truth of it, relate it to your own life, and remember the key question: *What's going on?*

2. EVALUATION

Remember that old Johnny Carson setup: "How cold is it, Johnny?" His answer was always some hilarious riff, "It's so cold that they turned the thermostats up in hell," or some such line. That's how I sometimes refer to the concept of evaluation. To evaluate is to appraise something, to rate it, to determine its intensity. The actor, having understood the event, should next evaluate the scene or moment. For example, how much does the junkie need dope? How determined is Hamlet to get revenge? How intent is Javier Bardem's hit man in *No Country For Old Men* on finding Josh Brolin? Without an evaluation of the scene or moment, the actor is lost as to what specific choices to make, what to play, what to look for in his own experience. In order to know what to play in a scene, the actor must understand the degree to which the character is experiencing a particular emotion or behavior, so that the proper choice can be made to fulfill that judgment. How much does Juliet want to be with Romeo? It is important to spur your character's life with a decision, with an evaluation. *How badly is this breakup affecting me? I'm sick about it!* Or, on the other side, *How badly do I want out of this relationship? I can't wait to be free!*

When you take a trip in life, it is always smart to ask the temperature of the city you are going to visit; then you know what clothes to bring in order to be comfortable. The same in acting. This can be difficult at times for certain actors—to know the temperature of the scene, or to hit the proper level of evaluation. They're playing a moment where they discover their spouse is cheating on them—they know it needs a higher, evaluated response, but they're stuck somehow. No juice. They just can't hit it. Often I'll advise the actor in this case to "assume the position," like when a cop says, "Get out of the car and assume the position." We all know what it's like when you get pulled over, and then if they ask you to get out of the car—whoa. You're in danger and you better do as you're told, right? Well in acting, when you have to achieve a certain evaluation, do as you're told, as if the police officer ordered you. Assuming the position means you go directly to belief and experience without censoring or questioning —as a tool to spark your imagination, your involvement. The real emotions may be right there, just underneath. What you express when you assume the position is totally up to you—be free, really allow yourself to go. Don't censor or be critical of whatever impulses you get. It's a technique to free you from getting stuck in some moment in a scene.

An actor who has evaluated a scene or a moment properly is not necessarily yelling, slamming doors, and throwing things across the stage in some kind of manufactured rage. Remember a time you were so emotional that you couldn't speak? I once got mugged in front of my apartment building, and as the guys took my money I was cool as a cucumber. No reaction. Seemingly no fear. Almost relaxed about it. I walked up to my apartment, looked down and realized I had slightly pissed in my pants out of fear. Or the time I was on a date with a girl, and the chemistry was so strong between us that as we sat down at a restaurant and looked over the entrees, the menus in our hands were quietly shaking.

Many people have had the experience of almost being in a car wreck—missing it by inches. They're calm as they swerve to avoid crashing, and then five minutes later they can't breathe and are shaking. So always look to see how your evaluation manifests itself in emotions, and most importantly in behavior. Look to your life to understand better what to do as an actor.

3. BEHAVIOR

What is the character doing physically in the scene? What is the character's life, and how does the physical behavior affect that life? Is she writing a letter in the scene? Is she changing clothes? Is he cleaning up the room? People behave, they do things. One of my teachers stressed that you don't come on stage to do a scene, you enter to do something in a room. Often actors stand around and wait for their cues. But what is happening in the scene physically? Find out and do it. Experiment with different physical activities, create a physical life until you find the right one. If you look for what the character is doing physically and play that, instead of coming on the stage to do the lines, you will find all kinds of exciting things to act.

I once directed a scene in class from *Mary, Queen of Scots*. The actors had been stuck for where to place the scene, and seemed at a loss for what to do during the scene. What could their behavior be? I got the idea of playing the scene in a stable, and I even built a horse out of a shopping cart, found objects, and some fabric. The actress washed down the horse, brushed it. The actor calmed and talked to the horse when it "moved." That horse—built overnight with no money, wheels showing underneath the bottom of the fabric—gave the scene a life that wasn't present before.

In a scene I directed from *Klute*, I had the Bree Daniels character take a shower in front of Klute—this lent a flirtation, a seductiveness to the actress playing the scene. Excite the detective, turn him on, so that then he would give her the tapes she wanted. So here we have event: the **apparent event** of flirtation, the **actual**

event of her desperately wanting the tapes; **evaluation**—how badly does she want those tapes? Enough to seduce him? Absolutely. This leads to **behavior**: the choice of showering in front of him, which activates the emotional desperation of this character—a working call girl.

In Zeffirelli's film production of *Romeo and Juliet,* Romeo's problem in the balcony scene was physical: how to get up the vines, over the branches, and onto the balcony with Juliet. This physical life gave the scene humor, youth, and a touching humanity.

Here, for example, is how the great Russian director and teacher Stanislavski counsels his actors to create the chain of physical actions in the scene from *Othello* where Othello and Desdemona are together the morning after their nuptial night, before any shadow has crossed their love:

> *How should an actor live that scene? What line should he follow? Is it the line of love, of passion (that is, of feelings), the character line, the literary line, the storyline? No, it is the line of action, the line of truthful actions and of genuine confidence in them.*
>
> *Here is the line of physical actions: (1) Try to find Desdemona and kiss her as quickly as possible; (2) She is enjoying herself and is coy with Othello; the actor must fall in with her playfulness and joke lightheartedly with her, (3) On the way, Othello has met Iago and, in a good mood, has jested with the latter, (4) Desdemona has come back to draw Othello over to the couch and he, again playful with her, follows her; (5) They lie down, remain that way; let your wife fondle you and, insofar*

*as possible, respond in the same way. Thus,
the actor lives through five of the simplest
physical tasks.*

In other words, the actor performs physical tasks by
means of the simplest words and deeds, and follows
these tasks to a full emotional involvement. If you follow
the pattern of physical actions under the given
circumstances and you believe in them, don't worry, your
acting is headed in the right direction.

In Stanislavski's words again:

*A few dozen tasks and physical acts, that's how
you have to master your part...that's my advice
to you in preparing a part.*

"The job of the director is to turn psychology into
behavior." That's Kazan. The actor seeks to understand
or uncover for himself the psychology of the scene—
what's happening, what's there, *what's going on* in the
deepest sense, then creates the behavior that he thinks
will illuminate that. Brando in *Streetcar:* That dinner
scene, the way Blanche and Stella are making fun of him
and dismissing him as he eats, the psychology of how a
man like Kowalski would respond to that, leading to
behavior: his smashing the plates and saying the classic
line, "My place is cleared, you want me to clear yours?"
Or it could be something simple: reading, or getting
ready for bed, or eating—living and behaving in the
space, and thus finding a quiet truth to the moment.
Remember the specifics of living and behaving: the
particulars of going to bed, brushing one's hair, putting
on a robe, eating a cracker, taking off makeup, applying
that new special face cream. The specific task should be
of interest to the actor, so that she becomes absorbed in

the task: the specifics of applying this special face cream, massaging certain areas of the face, the gentle dabbing of Kleenex, checking it all in the mirror. A fine actress could do wonders with just this one behavior.

So don't go just by rote. Really involve yourself in the physical behavior, believe in it and participate. If she is eating, really eat. If he is cleaning a gun, really clean it. If you are involved and interested, the audience will be, too—they will be convinced of your reality. You will be more a person, more the character, and in a much better position to discover the truth of the moment. Actors stand around and talk the lines. People behave.

4. PHYSICAL / EMOTIONAL STATE

In what condition is the character? Drunk? Tired? Hungry? Hot? Cold? What effect does this physical state have on the character in the scene? In the movie, *Dog Day Afternoon,* the particular kind of exhaustion, restlessness, tension, and frayed nerves created by the actors added to the suspense of the film. It's like staying up for many hours studying or working: you get tired, but you also become hypertense and nervous. This kind of correctly chosen tiredness can lead you to fresh discoveries in the scene. So again, evaluation plays a major part in the selection of the proper physical state. Drunkenness. But what kind of drunkenness? Is it just a buzz or is it falling down? Is it the drunkenness of Joe Pesci's character in *Goodfellas*—violent, volatile, dangerously humorous? Is it the despairing pain, the drinking-to-forget, desperately-joking Jamie in *Long Day's Journey Into Night*? Is it the silly, farcical, loopy English actress in *California Suite*? One needs to select specifically what state, the degree of that state, and the characteristics of that state you will emphasize to suit the scene and the character.

In the rape scene in *Streetcar*, Stanley has what might be called a sexual drunk. The booze heightens his feeling for sex. This drunkenness affects the actor in every way: body, desire, freedom, sexual drive. Even the beer is popped from the bottle and squirted in the air like a sexual orgasm.

Sometimes the actor can easily decide the physical state of the character. Other times it must be explored in rehearsal, re-evaluated, changed, tried again until the appropriate state can be found. Take the drunkenness in the scene between two brothers in O'Neill's *Long Day's Journey Into Night*: The older brother is funny and pathetic at the start, but later, as a drinker is apt to do, he descends into despair and violence. It helps the actor enormously to create the specific physical state, and the particular behavior that comes from that state, and tie it into the scene. Heat, in a play like *Cat on a Hot Tin Roof* is not just heat, but a particular kind of heat that adds to the frustration and sexuality of the characters. If you have ever visited a humid, hot climate like the American South in summer or the Caribbean, you have felt the oppressive heat that makes even the most mundane daily task difficult. Even trying to put on your watch is annoying. The physical state strongly affects the behavior of a character, so when you choose, make it a real choice, an alive choice that will affect you specifically in the scene in a way that will involve you and illuminate the life of your character.

Pain is also a physical state. At the end of *On the Waterfront*, Brando is badly beaten up in a fight. He creates a full physical state of pain, dizziness, almost unable to stand. The drama becomes about whether he can walk to the dockworkers' gate. If he does, his side wins. His struggle to walk through his physical state of pain becomes the action, theme, and resolution of the film. The director, influenced by the physical life of the actor, makes a subjective camera of the dizzy, spinning, off-balance vision of the hero. We see what Brando sees for a moment. This is a masterfully realized physical state influencing all departments of the production.

Are you doing a scene that takes place in a hot climate? Rehearse at least once in a sauna—sounds wild, I know, but try it and observe what happens to you, how you behave. Then bring that behavior and sensory awareness to the rehearsal hall. A scene at the beach? Go to the beach. Be aware of the sand, the heat, the sound of the ocean. Bring this to your rehearsal. In *The Exorcist,* William Friedkin ensured the set was cold enough that you could see the actors' breath—the simple truth of the cold room helped the actors really believe in the power of the possessed girl to create that frigid environment.

Physical state is often closely linked to emotional state. Triggers in the immediate environment can spark memories and imagination that in turn affect you emotionally. Everyone knows the feeling when they hear a piece of music and think back to the romantic relationship they were in at the time—it can seem so present and real just from hearing the music. Or the aroma of perfume. Or seeing a certain photograph or painting, or the smell of certain flowers. There's an endless stream of sensations that can flood your system from the life around you—and as an actor you can help yourself by placing that photograph, those flowers, that piece of music on the set as you work.

But if he needs further assistance, the actor can investigate his past and isolate specific "sense memory" experiences, using imagination and concentration alone to create a particular sensation: heat around the face, pain in the right side, a headache around the temples— or the emotions that then follow from these sensations. My own take on sense memory is that we all have it, it's not a fancy idea. If that special music isn't available for my scene, I can concentrate on imagining it, and so excite my feelings about it, hum the melody softly to myself to coax the emotional experience. Sense memory can be overworked, too heavily emphasized in the acting arsenal, with endless exercises that can introvert some actors, or make those who aren't good at the exercise question their real acting talent. It becomes a kind of overdone game, too heavy on the going over and over the exercise to draw out a particular emotion, and if it's not perceived as being done satisfactorily, repeating it more and more. Sometimes this repeating becomes a grind toward an abstract perfection of the exercise, and in my opinion, can lead to an indulgence that may not bring results in truly improving the creativity or fulfillment of the actor.

As a young director, I would sometimes hire actors from class who were terrific in all these exercises—but then when they actually dealt with the story, the life of the scene, they couldn't cut it. Conversely, there are very fine actors who aren't able to execute this memory exercise. So it's a tool—some have an aptitude for it, and some don't. What's important is the *imagination.* I think for many actors, you just need to put your attention slightly on that memory, the music, the sensation, and the imagination can come alive. Maybe, as Juliet, you don't feel quite connected to your Romeo.... Think of your own romantic music, invite it in, be affected by it to whatever degree, and then move on.

So I believe the actor should first study the source material: the actual senses. In your life, just be aware of how you respond to certain physical elements and stimuli. The sun on your face. The wonderful smell of new mown grass. The screeching sound of car tires from a sudden stop. A toothache. Take note of these sensations, but don't dwell on it, don't overwork it. As you act, just let the slight sensation from this memory propel yourself into belief, and excite your imagination. In this way, the sensation you get from sense memory acts as a springboard to your imagination and belief. Belief leads to involvement. Let the smallest sensation be the fertile seed for the full realization of a complete physical or emotional state.

5. WHAT HAPPENED BEFORE THE SCENE?

An actor sits offstage before his entrance, and one of his compatriots takes a bucket of water and douses him with it. Why? Because the writer said that it was raining outside, and by choosing to make that experience very real, the actor was propelled into the scene with a life. So find the means to create whatever specific experience you need before coming into the scene. And while hopefully you won't need the bucket of water too often, your performance life must be continuous. Don't walk in like an actor coming from offstage, but rather as a person coming from *somewhere*. The famous acting couple, Alfred Lunt and Lynn Fontanne, were once in a production of Chekhov's *The Seagull* where they literally sat and ate a meal offstage in order to give themselves the reality of having just eaten dinner before entering.

In my production of *Streamers*, the actor Charles Durning was doing the last drunk scene in rehearsal when the idea occurred to him—that as he entered the scene, it was a continuation of the life he'd had prior to his entrance: walking down the road in a drunken stupor and telling the story of his day to a tree, a bush, a passing dog. When he entered the stage, he just kept his distracted conversation going and didn't relate to the other men in the barracks. This heightened the experience very much, giving his character a lost and disconnected quality. And when I directed Joan Hackett in *Call Me By My Rightful Name,* I had her rehearse a specific entrance—she was coming inside from the frigid cold of Riverside Drive in winter. I lived on Riverside Drive—so I knew only too well what that brutal, wind-driven cold was like. According to what the stage manager told me afterwards, I had her do the entrance 32 times in one rehearsal, relentlessly (and hopefully with charm) trying to find that bitter-ass cold I knew well. The behavior I wanted was that this specific cold made her snuggle seductively in the big coat we gave her, and she could look properly delicious to Robert Duvall, who was surprised and bowled over by her arrival in the room.

But an actor trying to particularize the moment before the scene need not be tied just to a physical state. Sometimes your character might be arriving from a devastating emotional event, such as being fired from a job, a severe fight or breakup with a loved one, the death of a friend or family member. There's a specificity to creating that emotional state, believing in it, being involved with it, and allowing it really to affect the actor, so they can in turn bring that life to the scene. If you fully nail the moment before, every nuance of the scene you now play will be affected because of this preparation.

Whether wet from the rain, dazed by an accident, angry from a previous argument, or grieving a loss, the actor must deal in detail and specifics so the performance will be affected by the life the actor brings on stage with him. That way, your life on stage or before the camera will have a sense of continuing behavior rather than the artificial sense of just coming on to play the scene.

6. CREATIVE HIDING

In a hospital, a doctor approaches the father of a young child.

DOCTOR: Sir, your daughter ....

FATHER *(As he looks away, down at his shoes, unable to face the news, moving a scrap of paper with his foot)*: Is she going to be okay?

DOCTOR: For sure. She's going to be just fine.

Or, a different scene: You're driving through a rural community, and you need directions. You pull to the side of the road where there is a man with a beard, wearing overalls, whittling a piece of wood in his hands.

YOU: Excuse me, do you know where there's a bed & breakfast?

MAN *(Continuing to whittle, he doesn't even look up at you):* You gotta go down that road there and make a left at the fork. *(He barely moves his head in the direction of the road.)*

Many characters that we play do not have the ability or the inclination at a given moment to confront another character directly. They feel too angry, tearful, sensual, wrought up. Or perhaps they're the kind of person who doesn't confront directly, tends to hide, never looks a person in the eye. An actor can sometimes find the truth of the moment by dealing with something else in the scene rather than confronting the other character. This technique can help in two ways: 1) by covering the emotion, hiding it—as people often do in life—you then behave more like a real person, and 2) by playing away from your partner—as the father did by looking at his feet, or as the man did carving that wood—you create behavior, which is the major thrust of the actor's work.

Creative hiding during moments of high emotion can allow the actor to release and express feelings more deeply, because by hiding they deflect those feelings, as people do. This activity becomes a kind of mask that reveals more than it conceals. The boss has to tell you about a tragic phone message concerning a member of your family, and in telling you about it, he can't look at you, but continues to fiddle with the paperweight on his desk. In playing the boss in this scene, you would find yourself more expressive, more fully emotional, by dealing with the paperweight rather than openly addressing the victim of the terrible news. Creative hiding is a human instinct to protect, to hide one's feelings during duress. By using this technique, tapping into this wellspring of human behavior, the actor connects with a truthful part of life.

I had a very emotional scene once in a room with someone. It was difficult for me to face that person with the intense grief I was experiencing, so as the tears rolled down my cheeks I looked out the window, not allowing her to see my face. I "played" the carpet, the plants in the room, the view outdoors, the trees, the grass, the cars on the street. As I played off of those things, more of my feelings came out, because I protected myself from her gaze. The audience understands this kind of behavior because they have experienced it, even if they don't label it creative hiding. So use this technique in your rehearsals—particularly if you have a scene with high emotionality, or with a character who you have determined tends not to confront the people he's dealing with so head-on. Don't play everything to your partner. Find ways to use creative hiding, and see what this does to your acting.

7. BE A PERSON

Each character you play is a person—simple to say, yes, but the creation of a real person is difficult. You're trying to be a person, not an actor. But many actors miss the fact that they themselves are people—they don't use the valuable resources of their own sensations, their own experience, their own behavior. They don't observe the behavior of friends and family they've known their whole lives, the behavior of people they see around them every day. So they approach their work from an attitude of trying to "figure out" acting and make hot "acting" choices. But remember the main thrust is to be a person. In the scene, what would a person do?

Look at the six-o'clock news some time. A disaster hits some neighborhood or small town, and the reporter sticks a microphone in the face of a man who just lost his home—what does this man do? Often you will see no emotion whatsoever. He will speak very calmly about the tornado that just destroyed his life. There's a hint of emotion in his voice. He speaks very clearly and calmly. Suddenly he stops in the middle of a word, unable to continue. An actor, given this script, might automatically look for the chance to jump with his emotions, break down in sobs because that seems the obvious choice for someone who just lost his home. But a person often will have totally different reactions from those of an actor. A person often tries not to cry—an actor too often cries.

Actors sometimes jump at the chance to play a huge response to some big news. One character says to another, "You just won a million dollars!" And the actor immediately jumps up and down and yells about winning a million dollars. But what would a person do? Stanislavski spoke of reflective delay. There is often a delay as a person processes information—whether it's very good or very bad. Think back to a time in your life when some big news was delivered. What did you do? Did you immediately jump up and down, scream with joy or pain? Did you leap to an emotional response? Or did you just sit down for a moment, saying nothing? Did you question the information, or even insist that it wasn't true? How long did it take to really understand that you won that award before you responded? That a loved one died? That you got into the college of your choice?

Be a person. Don't just go for the emotion or the obvious response. Think about the behavior of people interviewed on the six-o'clock news. Reflective delay. Check out your life and remember what you did specifically in a particular circumstance—observe how a person responds and let that always be your guide.

8. INNER AND OUTER LIFE: THE "COVER"

*"...A woman's charm is fifty percent illusion,
but when a thing is important I tell the truth,
and this is the truth: I haven't cheated my sister
or you or anyone else as long as I have lived."*

In *A Streetcar Named Desire,* Blanche DuBois is
terrified, anxious, holding a lot of grief inside. These
feelings surface many times, yet on the outside she plays
the coquettish Southern Belle, all sweetness and light.
As the actress understands the inner and outer life, she
is able to play beautifully between the two, allowing the
inside to affect the outside, and back again. This leads
her to feel compassion and understanding for the fully
realized Blanche, and to render a more moving
portrayal. The understanding and acting out of the inner
and outer life, and how one affects the other, will lead
you to the truth of what's actually going on with a
character. This bounce, if you will, between inner and
outer life, is what takes place with a real person.

Work on inner and outer life is linked tightly with
"subtext," which is a very important concept in acting—
here's my own definition:

> **subtext**, n., a stream of consciousness flowing
> often beneath the character's awareness, but
> always having a strong effect on what he or she
> wants, feels and does.

The actor has to discover this subtext, nail it, and then
connect with this somewhat buried or hidden thought
and emotion, use it to propel the character's life. Subtext
is the underlying truth of what a character is thinking or
doing, the inner life.

People often "cover" their feelings, their inner life, with a very contrary outer life. Knowing this well, actors will many times tell me how they wanted to "play the cover"—meaning their outer life was calm but they intended the inner life to be rich with emotion or anger or romantic desire. Too often, however, they've put a cover on nothing—akin to putting a lid on a pot of water, but forgetting to turn on the burner. You cannot "play the cover" of a placid exterior without understanding and investigating the inner emotions that are being covered. My solution to this common problem is ensure the actor's chosen inner life *really exists*—bring it out and play the inner life during rehearsal in a very overt way. Make the inner life alive and on fire. Then cover it. This generally brings more depth to the character's life.

When Brando in *Sayonara* enters the scene where he expects to find the bodies of his two dear friends, his face is a stoic, protective mask, holding back the strong emotions and anxiety that he feels inside. These two feelings, coexisting in conflict, in tension—feeling a great deal, but trying to hold on to himself—give this moment its truth and full theatrical expression. At the end of *Sense and Sensibility,* when Hugh Grant's character arrives to say he is finally available to Emma Thompson's—she broke into convulsive sobs of joy and relief, a terrific example of an actress using inner and outer life: that inner life of passion and desire finally overtaking the very serene, 19th century proper English social outer life.

People's lives are sometimes so painful, they need a social mask or humor to endure. As actors, you need to understand both sides fully, and play the beautiful game that exists between the two, inner and outer life, as they evolve through the story.

9. WHO'S THE AUTHOR?

I once directed a comedy on Broadway where there were some cryptic one-liners I didn't quite know how to handle. There was one particular moment where one of those one-liners fell dead in rehearsal, then also at the previews. At some point during previews I went to a dinner party with the author, and he dominated the evening with one great one-liner after another. He had this incredible throw-away manner, which brought huge laughs from the other guests, and as I watched, studied him, I got it. Don't punch the one-liners. Throw them away. It was deceptively simple, but seeing this writer handle humor this way gave me the understanding of how to direct the actor in his work. I got him to throw away the line, and like magic, the audience roared.

So who wrote the piece? This question is too often overlooked by actors. Is it Woody Allen? Bertolt Brecht? Tennessee Williams? Every author has their own style, their own sense of humor, their own point-of-view. This can affect the choices you make as an actor. The kind of drunk you would play in a frathouse movie like *Animal House* is different from what you would play for Eugene O'Neill. It's not that one of them is "more real" than the other, but the frathouse movie has a certain sensibility— wild, young, sexually charged, broadly comedic—and O'Neill a very different one—a deep, chronic, emotional and possessed kind of drunk. You have to be aware of the difference. If you're playing in a farce like *Noises Off,* then the palette of choices you have as an actor is vastly different from the palette for *Macbeth,* because *Noises Off*'s zany world is quite a contrast from Shakespeare's dramatic pathology. Perhaps the contrast between *Noises Off* and *Macbeth* is too stark, too obvious, but it's only to make clear that the issue of *Who's The Author?* needs the actor's special attention.

Here's a step far too often ignored: *Read other works by the author.* What are they after in their writing? Really investigate. Dig. Figure out the sensibility through their other plays and films. Or perhaps you're dealing with a first-time author—if that's the case, they're probably available! Go out with them, meet them, go to a party as I did with that guy whose work I was directing. Try to nail down the humor, the intelligence, the point of view so you understand their writing. One way or another, get to know and be influenced by the writer. You've observed the phenomenon of certain authors who use the same actors again and again—this is because the actor *understands* them, their way, their voice, their style.

10. IMPROVISATION

I can't mention this word in class without its being instantly linked by many of my students to "improv comedy." I have embarked umpteen times on hour-long class discussions regarding this misunderstanding. I'm not putting down improv comedy—I think entertainment is great, I love to laugh as much as the next guy, and some fine actors have come from an improv background. But improv comedy is often not strictly improvisation, as it ends up blending with sketch writing that is pointed towards getting a laugh. Improv and sketch comedy can help to create comedic actors, but the potential downside is that it can emphasize and cement in the actor a kind of glibness that keeps things on the surface, shallow, not fully realized.

To me, improvisation is rooted in theatre history—the ageless struggle to make the dialogue real, spontaneous, as though spoken for the first time.

That method of acting, I say, which makes the words seem like a passage learned by rote, must be avoided and endeavor must be made above all other things to render whatever is spoken thoroughly effective, with suitable alteration of tones and appropriate gestures. The whole dialogue must seem like a familiar talk, wholly improvised.

Leone di Somi, Italian playwright
and director (1527-1592)

Improvisation is a tool that I believe can help break down a clichéd, mechanical, by-rote rendering of a scene; it can throw the actor off balance, breaking him out of a lifeless expression. If you as an actor are frozen in the scene, improvisation can help release you from mechanical responses, freeing you to explore new choices, fresh insights, concepts that surprise you, your acting partners, and the audience.

improvisation, n. A course pursued in accordance with no previously devised plan, policy, or consideration. Sudden, unforeseen, unexpected. To bring about, arrange, make on the spur of the moment without preparation.

Here are some ways you can use improvisation to help you in your work:

Play the written scene, but use your own words to paraphrase the text. This can be particularly useful with an author like Shakespeare, where the nature of the language can be a real obstacle. But even contemporary authors may use words or phrasing that feel uncomfortable to you. Go ahead. Rehearsal is a free-fire zone—say it your way. Do what you need to do to discover the real intent of the communication. Then work your way back to the text using that understanding you gained through improvisation. It is a good idea when returning to the scene as written to keep improvising a bit. You get back into the script gradually, rather than all at once.

Set up a situation *analogous* to the written scene. Let's say the written scene is about an employee leaving a job where the boss has been a real mentor to him. You could improvise a different kind of breakup, a son or daughter leaving home to go on their own, or perhaps even a romantic breakup. Improvise a scene with that subtext, so you can freely explore and uncover wonderful layers of behavior and emotional expression without the constraint of the written scene. Now go back to the scene. That employee/employer relationship will be a bit richer, more lively, the lines less predictable.

Explore a part of the story that is not included in the script, but relates to your scene. Let's say you have a script about a couple getting divorced. The early moments of the relationship are not in the script. Here you could improvise the first date between them, or the incredible romance of the proposal. I did this once when working on *Cat on a Hot Tin Roof,* in which the relationship between Brick and Maggie is perilously strained. I had the actors improvise a picnic where Brick proposed to her. The exercise was pretty quick. Maybe 10-15 minutes. Then back to the scene—the love that was now being rejected by Brick was much greater than before. So this kind of improvisation gives you and your partner the one thing that every character has more of than the actor playing him: a sense of the experience and history that the character has lived. You can develop that history through improvisation. This will add depth to your performance and enhance your experience with the other actors in your project.

Another technique is to use gibberish improv, where you say what you mean in a nonsensical language, or just sounds. This incites you to be more expressive, out of a deeper part of your talent. It gets you away from what Stanislavski called "the muscle of the tongue," relying too much on the words. In addition, your acting partner now must really look at your body language and listen for any innuendos in the timbre of your voice to get an understanding of what is being communicated. He needs really to respond to you as the gibberish-talker, rather than merely listen for a cue.

Find the mistakes. Use improvisation by being alert and utilizing a "mistake" on stage, either in rehearsal or performance, to enhance the actor's work: a letter is dropped, a glass falls and breaks, someone has difficulty putting on a coat. From the smallest to the largest mistake, the really fine actor should be able to use them as a springboard for further creative exploration. You should respond to a mistake as a person would—not be stuck by the fact that this mistake never happened in rehearsal. The director William Wyler would wait through many takes for one such mistake that would catch the actor off guard, and create a fresh reaction.

Improvisation is used as a tool to free creativity in many art forms. Musicians (especially in jazz) take off on a given theme to find new avenues of expression. But even

Arthur Schnabel, the great classical pianist and interpreter of Beethoven, would sometimes deviate from the written score in an effort to express the music more powerfully, more personally. Painters often follow a free, unimpeded flow of color or form in order to discover new expressions. In the cases of Pollock, de Kooning, and Picasso, these flights of fancy often became their style, forming the very structure of their work.

This tradition of improvisation goes back to the *commedia dell'arte* and is used in contemporary work such as in the creation of *A Chorus Line, Hatful of Rain,* and many more recent films such as *Secrets and Lies* by the director Mike Leigh, who uses improvisation almost exclusively in writing his scripts. So feel free—improvise away, so as to find the author's and your own truth.

(See also the Improvisation Exercise in the chapter **"Class Exercises"** for more on this topic.)

11. HUMOR

An actor comes home one day to find his house is a mess. Furniture has been overturned, everything is in a shambles. He runs upstairs to find his wife slumped on their bed, bruised and disheveled, weeping terribly. The actor rushes over and asks her, "Honey, what happened?" His wife answers, "Your agent. He came over here this afternoon—it was horrible. He was violent, he wrecked the house, and then he raped me!" The actor, eyes bugging out from shock, responds with reverence, "My *agent* was here?"

I'm always on the hunt for a good joke, and this one about the actor is one that I love. But humor is not just a joke or a funny line. What is humor exactly? And why is it important for the actor? Actually, why is it a *must* for the actor?

> **humor**, n., the ability to perceive, enjoy or express what is amusing, comical, incongruous or absurd.

> **irony**, n., a form of expression in which an intended meaning is the opposite of the literal meaning of the words used.

> **wit**, n., the natural ability to perceive and express, in an ingeniously humorous manner, the relationship between seemingly unrelated things. *Wit has truth in it, wisecracking is simply calisthenics with words* —Dorothy Parker

The joke above allows the world and the actor to laugh, and then see the self-centeredness of actors. Humor is a point of view that allows one to realize and laugh at the ridiculousness of life. Try to play Hamlet without humor—it will be boring and impossible to endure.

One of the real stumbling blocks is the exaggerated significance that actors place on serious scenes. Their attitude or way of expression becomes stiff, overly dramatic, and thus often dull and repetitive. You want to say, "Enough, already!" The introduction of humor is a person's way of trying to endure life, to not be so maudlin and martyred. Ladies and gentlemen, suffering needs the relief of humor. Mothers, please pay special attention!

My friend, the late Michael Shurtleff, a well-known playwright and casting director, said, "One would sometimes think actors are trying to reverse the life process by what they do when they act. They take humor out instead of putting it in. We have trouble believing a performance that has no humor. It is unlike life. The more serious the situation, the more we need humor to endure it."

John F. Kennedy once said, "I am the man who accompanied Jacqueline Kennedy to Paris." There is an intelligence, an irony there that is so delicious. Quality humor and irony comes from that certain intelligence. It can't just be one-liners or sight gags. Humor should reveal something to us, point out a facet of life that was unseen or perhaps feared or avoided. JFK may well have been put off by the fact that Paris went crazy more for his wife than for him—but the way he phrased it makes us laugh at the truth and makes clear that he maintained his dignity and intelligence.

12. TRUST

Hanging from a cliff, holding a thin, frayed rope—the rope seems to be giving way, thinner and thinner.... High above the ground, the rope seems ready to snap! That's an artist as he takes dangerous risks. So what does this risk-taking seeming-madman need? More governmental support. No, just kidding. He needs trust. The confidence that all will be fine—that his risky choice will work. Trust. Trust. Trust must be your mantra, your key, the flying trapeze net. Fly, try, seem to die, but don't be afraid—trust. Without trust, there can be no life, no art.

> **trust**, n., a feeling of emotional security, resulting from faith in oneself. A firm belief in one's powers, abilities or capacities.

You must know that any art that is worth its salt is a high-wire act, a cliff-hanger, a risk, a chance—so...that's right, you got it: Trust. Trust your director, your writer, your acting partners, your teacher, and don't forget your agent, but mostly...? Yeah, always trust yourself.

The great Anthony Quinn said that doubt and fear were his best friends—because they pushed him to find the truth, the answers to a character or a scene. Okay—if fear pushes you forward to explore more, that's good. Insecurities are a part of any creative process, but don't allow doubts to override your choices and creative work. Doubt, if it stops you in your tracks, is to be overcome with...that's it. Yeah, you got it. We're singing the same song.

13. BEING PERSONAL

"Poor Rosa." That was the only line found in one of the scripts of the great Italian actress, Eleanor Duse. I think it means she really understood the role, really felt for Rosa, identified with her. The two simple words, "Poor Rosa," were all Duse needed to be personal. So what does it mean to "be personal" in acting? It's talked about a lot, but I feel the term is often misunderstood, misinterpreted.

> **personal**, *adj.*, 1. monogrammed with one's name or initials, 2. individually owned, 3. inwardly felt, 4. close to one's heart, 5. *In acting:* being affected by and allowing yourself to experience specifically what the character is going through on an emotional level.

Macbeth has to murder the king. He decides to do it, reluctantly. This is a kind of wild, not-easily-dealt-with, unusual circumstance. What must an actor do to make this event personal? He must determine the emotional state and behavior of the character, and then crawl his way into that experience. He has to get under Macbeth's skin, feel the adrenaline, the fevered pulse, the panic of the reluctant murderer that Shakespeare wrote. The personal actor wants to get close to that feeling and understand it. He seeks out the behavior and emotional state, the personal connection, with his own blood, sweat, and tears. Stanislavski spoke of the "magic if"— *What if I had the experience of this character? What would I do? How would I feel?* The personal actor is on a quest for the answer to that "magic if."

But note that I have not said the personal actor, being, say, from Texas, chooses that his Macbeth is from Houston. This is where actors seeking to be personal sometimes err. It's not your personal biography that does the trick. It's your personal feelings, your body, your physical responses that are needed. Nor does being personal mean you choose that the character's personality is just like yours, particularly if by doing so you evade qualities necessary for the story. So if you're a cool customer, an unflappable type, then it would also be a mistake to make your Macbeth this very cool person who doesn't flinch at murder. Because Macbeth does— he flinches. So there's the story—story is king, it can never be left out. Being personal is applying your emotions, your body, your physical responses, your blood, sweat and tears *to a very specific story.* An unflappable Macbeth from Houston may not satisfy our old friend William.

One time when I was directing a play, I had the problem that the two lead actors were not exactly into each other. It was affecting the chemistry of the couple in the play— I felt the coldness between them in the performances.

Not good for a love story! So, I went to the actor and told him that the girl was a little cold because in fact she had a crush on him, and felt weird about it. Then I told the same thing to the actress about the leading man. Naughty of me, no? But it worked. Suddenly they were both affected by each other, the adrenaline was flowing between the two actors, and the play clicked from there on out.

I often say, "You are stuck with the character, and the character is stuck with you." If you choose to connect a part of the story to the personal facts of your life, it's done to spark your emotions—in other words, these facts must move you *closer* to the character and the story, otherwise they're not relevant. Being personal doesn't mean infusing a character, say a sweet, unassuming guy, with the physical rage you personally are feeling at your agents and the people who won't cast you. Because unless you are able to take this rage, and cover it beautifully with the sweetness of the character, you will wreck the story about this unassuming guy.

The best acting requires personal *investment,* that you are personally *involved,* that somehow you are relating to the events of *this story* and letting them affect you in such a way that you leave the stage knowing that some part of you was left out there in service of the story. And perhaps that's not technical enough for some, but to me that's what being personal really is. *What did it cost you?* You are a prism. The light originates from the author and passes through you, and it's not just refracted, it is *changed* by having passed through you. Each different actor will change the light differently, and that's the magic of how your unique prism will create a true, personal experience in acting.

14. PATHOLOGY

Richard III. Is he Buddha's cousin? In *Hannah and Her Sisters*, are they all Sisters Theresa? In the works of Tennessee Williams, Arthur Miller, Shakespeare, David Mamet or Sam Shepard—do they have mostly delicate, innocent characters with no dark side? Is *The Price* about the meeting of the Archangel and St. Peter? Is *A View from the Bridge* about purity? No. Pathology abounds. I'm not advocating this condition as the answer to life. But as actors, you have to understand the morbid nature of many characters. As the medical pathologist studies the diseased cell in order better to understand the workings of the human body, the artist draws our attention to emotional pathology so that we may better understand the mind and spirit of a person. As an artist, you've got to probe and tap these pathologies within yourself or within your imagination or within your fantasies. Not to make yourselves sickos, not to make yourselves into neurotics, not to make yourself pathological. But to know how to play it. And there is for most characters a neurotic nature, isn't there? The best movie that I ever saw about Christ was Pasolini's movie, *The Gospel According to St. Matthew*. The actor plays him like a very troubled man. Very intense and violent, not just saintly. I don't know that all Christians like it, but it's very interesting. Of course, Christ's story was surrounded with pathology; illness, torture, healing, and death.

> **pathology**, n., **1.** that which applies to physical, mental or moral conditions that have their origin in disease or marked abnormality. (Dracula) **2.** a diseased mind subject to self-deception. (Blanche DuBois) **3.** a morbid fascination for crime, death, and violence. (Richard III) **4. pathological liar:** a person

who habitually tells lies so exaggerated and
bizarre that they are suggestive of mental
disorder. (Iago)

I had a student in New York one time—I really had it out
to bust this guy, because he was so damned spiritual. He
was almost like a virgin. Or maybe he was. He was so
pure. When he played the Yeshiva student in *Yentl*, he
was incredible: pure, wonderful, loving. But how many
roles are there like this? How many sweet, perfect beings
are walking around? I don't want to take somebody's
spirituality away from them in their life, but as an artist,
you have to be able to create many aspects of different
characters, some of those aspects associated with
pathology. Now, are we all like my spiritual friend in
New York? Nah. I don't think so. I'd bet just about all of
us have had a moment or maybe many moments where
we have confronted a darker side to our personality, one
not so shiny and polished and social. Right? C'mon admit
it, you've had a hairy moment or two in your life. Agreed?
Good, we can go on.

Pathology exists in comedies like *The Odd Couple* or
Chaplin or Laurel and Hardy—and in romance. There's
a certain pathology in romance. And sex. Look at the
greatest love story of all time: *Romeo and Juliet*. It isn't
just spiritual, saintly-sweet and romantic. Shakespeare
said love is a disease. All through the story—violence,
youthful rebellion, parental repression. Pathology. The
French have an expression for orgasm, *la petite mort,* the
little death. Pathology. It isn't just cross the bridge into
Romantic Paradise. Romeo and Juliet have one fervent
moment, they make it together, and he's gone. The next
time they meet is in the tomb, and they both die.
Pathology. Seek out its artistic influence on your

imagination and emotions, and let it into your characters.

Pathology is part of life, part of all literature. You have to look within and accept that part of yourself in acting, and know that when used in service of art, it's a gift. But you do have to be willing to admit that you're not this perfect angel. You have to be willing to remember the time you drank too much, or when you were exhausted and that placid demeanor cracked into a temper, or when you actually felt a real hatred for a rival or even a family member. Just remember what one of those Russian guys said: "If you can kill a fly, you can play Othello." These feelings are common to all of us at some point, and again, I'm not looking to drop you in an ocean of pathology and so into introversion. But a drop of the ocean is still the ocean, and that drop is enough to let you get close to the truth of a darker character, rather than sitting back and judging it from a moral high ground. Francis Bacon painted these feelings. Edgar Allan Poe wrote about them. And now, you may well be called upon to act them, and you mustn't flinch or be shy about it.

15. OBJECTIVES

Let's face it: We all know what it feels like to want something. Men with regard to certain automobiles can be quite a meditation on desire. Almost as ardent as a woman can be about that certain handbag. And then there are those concert tickets. The painting. That new gadget. A wristwatch. And of course, that woman. Or that man. The thought of acquiring the desired item becomes incessant, part of the moment to moment of your lives, often thought about quite feverishly. And yet, it's not like you're drooling either. Drooling and being stupid isn't going to get you what you want. But the pulse races, the mind obsesses, the concentration is focused by desire. This is a lot of what I want to say about objectives. We all know innately what it is to want something, to chase something, to go after something— that's what I mean by objectives: what the character is going after.

Your job as an actor is quickly to identify this desire within the character. Every story is about someone wanting something, and the obstacles they overcome to achieve it. Usually this objective is easily spotted, and then it's a matter of firing up that desire within you so it's hot, so it affects you in your work with the role.

I think too much analytical effort is expended on this topic. I've seen actors get too caught up in these objectives, too stilted in acting them out. Remember, people often hide, cover what they want, pretend not to want what they are pursuing. Since I don't really push objectives so much in my teaching, actors sometimes ask me whether having a highly evaluated objective doesn't counter what I teach about simply being a person, which is more my kind of emphasis. No, I don't think so. To me, it's easy to place the proper emphasis on objectives, while still working always to be a person, to reveal a simple human life. For example: I'll bet all of you have had occasion to drive to a hotel or apartment for a tryst, either planned or improvised. *Desire, yes?* And sexual desire can be as obsessive as desire gets. But did you drive like a maniac? I don't think so. You don't want to get into an accident. You don't want a speeding ticket. You don't want that unnecessary delay or distraction or attention, you don't want anything to get in the way of your tryst. And yet the pulse is racing and the mind absorbed while you drive, yes, with some hot intention, but also carefully. To the observer in the car next to you, you may be just this very calm person driving a car, but the fever is there, underneath. The objective is sometimes hidden from view. When I was young, I would help my father when he came home, making him some tea, fetching his slippers, and offering warm, concerned conversation. My objective? Get the keys to the car!

So try to understand these objectives from a life standpoint. Observe yourself and others going after what they desire, and learn to translate these objectives in a human way from words into action. So watch out that you don't go on a head trip about objectives—it's not an academic exercise, but hopefully a simple analysis of what the character wants. That part is usually pretty easy. Then you have to ignite that fire within you so that as the concentration focuses on what you want, the pulse moves, the hands want to shake—now, in a very experiential way, you can deal with how you express the desire or objective: Cover it completely? Reveal it intimately? Scream it to the world? Or perhaps some piece of all of these as you act through the story.

16. SPECIFICS

A scene from the play, *Art,* was done recently in my class, with two very talented guys fighting it out and insulting each other deliciously. But yet the scene didn't quite work. There was a set full of furniture there, but I joked with them afterwards that I wanted to send a crew up on stage as they acted to remove the furniture. They weren't using it. Replace the couch and the bar with lecterns, and maybe it would have worked—it was more of a debate than a real fight. They stood across from each other and hurled witty remarks. It was funny, but it wasn't *specific.* They weren't *specifically* affecting each other as much as they should have. Nor was the set *specifically* used by either of them. It wasn't really anyone's apartment.

The night before, two actors in another class were doing a scene from *It Happened One Night,* and they wanted some rain. So they gave the whole front row of students in class some squirt bottles full of water, who aimed them high above the actors, and they played a good part of the scene under a cascade of droplets coming from the sky. I loved it. They wanted rain. They went and got rain. For about $12 in squirt bottles. They were specific about it, they achieved it, and it was delicious—the imagination, the fun of it.

Specifics relate to every aspect of the work, to every item on this checklist. The event: What, *specifically* is going on? At a Mafia wedding it isn't just throwing rice, it's about the favors asked of the Don. In *Girl on the Via Flaminia,* it's that she's a virgin—that specificity of event. Evaluation: How cold is it, Johnny? The humor of his response was in how specific it was. *So cold that a polar bear is wearing his mink.* So what is the specific evaluation? Or physical state: what kind of limp, or cold virus, or heat, or headache? You have to nail these things. You have to nail them specifically. A generality will leave you and the audience unmoved, unclear, uninvolved. The more specific you are, the more you and the audience gets drawn in to what you're creating.

A costume problem for an actor playing a bum: specifically what kind of bum? What kind of hat, what trousers, what vest? How soiled should his clothing be, and where did he find them? In a rich man's garbage can? In the trash bin of a thrift store? A specific choice is needed in professional work to reveal the individuality of this character. Brecht spoke about a young actor in his company, playing a homeless guy, who went nuts trying to find the costume—which jacket, which hat? The actor finally solved it by finding a toothbrush, and putting it in the breast pocket of his soiled jacket—that little specific prop gave the character a certain dignity the actor was looking for. And Kazan spoke of costuming—he said to look at "how people dress as an expression of what they wish to gain from an occasion. How their attire is an expression of each day's mood and hope." Specifics.

Or think of Peter Falk as *Columbo*—the choice of the raincoat and the old Peugeot. Those were Falk's own specific choices that he felt revealed the essence of this very unglamorous—yet very human—detective, and gave him a certain behavior, this down-to-earth guy who doesn't look as if he could be much of a threat, but in actuality is very much a threat. I like specific choices that lead to specific behavior, specific emotional responses. I don't like so-called "specifics" that get into unnecessary character biography: These tend to be academically oriented choices that exist only in the actor's head. Specifics need to exist in the fabric of the work, the behavior, the life on stage. If the only way I can know your specific choice is by your telling me about it after the fact—then I'll try to get you to make that specific choice clearer and more alive in the performance.

Specifics relate to training itself: If the actor has a speech problem, determine specifically what the problem is, then do vocal exercises selected to correct that problem. For a problem with physical tension, specify in what part of the body the tension lies, and release the tension in that area. Details. Specifics. Without them, you're dead as an actor—in training, in the work itself, in administration—all of it.

17. USE OF OBJECTS

I've broken down the use of objects into four categories:

1) **Simple physical objects:** *Here's a wine glass. It's empty. Where's the bottle? Ah there it is, let me go get that and refill my glass....*

I remember in my first scene as an actor at university, I had to deal with a wine glass as part of the scene. I was nervous, I was worried I would spill it, I wasn't natural at all. I just couldn't do it. So while simple physical objects, simple props, may seem an elementary topic, the fact is that the actor almost has to relearn how to use simple objects in his work. We use simple objects all day everyday, but actors have to make it seem natural under the duress of performance. So don't forget that people *do things.* Observe the conversations around you, and you'll see all sorts of behavior with coffee cups, eyeglasses, household items, phones, etc. Actors, on the other hand, often will just stand on stage and play the lines to each other. So go ahead, sit in that couch, live in it. Feel the weight of that glass. The texture. The configuration of the object. See something in the object you've never seen before. This will make you more alert, more alive in the moment of dealing with the objects, and therefore you will be more comfortable. Don't be afraid to surround yourself with objects and really use them. Use of simple physical objects gives your acting a behavioral foundation.

2) **Personal objects:** *Hey, this is my shaving gear. I know how to use this with my eyes closed. That's my makeup kit and mirror—I use that every day. I know where the latch catches and how it needs a little coaxing to open....*

Personal objects help the actor because using your own books, kitchen utensils, photographs, makeup kit, shaving gear, or the like helps you feel at home, doing real tasks, not make-believe. It's your own object, so you may connect to it in a much more personal way than if it were just a prop from the theatre. Personal objects can connect you with the life on stage because they're familiar, and so the tasks and your overall behavior become more natural.

3) **Personal emotional objects:** *Now here's a photograph of my father. This is something different. This takes me to another place. And here's my diary. Wow, did I really feel that way back then? The images are really flying now....*

Objects that have an emotional connection for the actor have been employed since theatre began. Remember the Greek actor from ancient times, who placed the ashes of his dead son on stage to feed him emotionally. Don't be limited by the author's use of objects; feel free to bring anything that helps you in the scene. In *The Three Sisters,* Chekhov has you speak of the longing to go to Moscow, but as you rehearse, the scene is dead for you. Then you bring a brooch that evokes deep memories, a longing emotion is triggered within you: the scene jumps to life. A personal emotional object can be the catalyst that sets off a chain of emotional reactions. Sometimes this personal object has so much power it becomes the scene itself. A friend of mine carries with him a buckeye, a polished seed from the buckeye tree about the size of a walnut in the shell. When he touches this seed in his jacket pocket, the texture of it triggers in him a memory of his brother on the bluffs over a Kentucky creek, carefree and adventurous. Now this memory makes him feel a terrible longing and sadness for his brother who, in later life, suffered a mental breakdown. Why he carries this buckeye with him, I don't quite understand, but it works every time.

4) Personal inner objects: *Okay, here I am at the audition—I wish I could bring some props in with me, but that's not practical. I need something to spark that emotion.... Hold on, I remember that necklace my grandmother gave me the last time I saw her, let me think on that for a moment. Yeah, now I feel it....*

As a child, I waited sometimes for hours for my uncle to come and take me with him on a trip. He owned a trucking company and as I saw him approach in the big red truck, I became excited as hell. Sometimes when he was running behind schedule, he would not stop but go speeding by. The feeling of uncontained joy as I saw him approach, as well as the feelings of sadness, anger, and real grief as he passed me by, are ones I have tapped into many times, merely by focusing and concentrating on that red truck, that inner object. Music can be a great catalyst for finding inner objects—it is often linked to specific places and events that trigger feelings you can use. Ditto with aromas—a certain perfume that reminds you of a person, and an experience you had with that person that is able to knock your socks off—all this is good fuel for an actor.

18. ARBITRARY CHOICES

In Sherwood Anderson's *Winesburg, Ohio*, a woman, seemingly sedate, repressed and in control, one rainy night dashes naked from her house and throws herself on the muddy lawn. Is this logical behavior? On the surface, no. But buried in the life experience of this character is a certain logic, revealed through this arbitrary behavior—a kind of rebellion—that becomes a wonderfully expressive example of how a potentially "illogical" action can often actually determine the truth of a moment.

Actors should learn to look for the arbitrary choice, which is an imaginative action that seems contrary to the logic of the scene or the character. So you see, using logic in acting should not limit you merely to choices that "make sense" on a surface level. Actors often will suppress such an impulse, however, as some voice within them warns, "The character wouldn't do that." Don't drop that choice so fast. Examine it and even act it out. See if you can work it into the story of your character— it could lead you to gold. As Juliet, you find yourself on a balcony with Romeo, and you have an impulse to kiss him passionately, and even aggressively want to seduce him. *Do it.* Don't think to yourself, "It wouldn't be logical for a prim, morally correct daughter of a strict family to kiss a stranger like this." Sometimes the given circumstance forces the character to do something quite different from what we, and even the character, expected. Be alert to the fact that a character's logic may seem at times illogical, even crazy. People often reveal themselves by doing the opposite of what you expect. Kazan: "Character is revealed through contradiction." Following the contradictory impulse is exciting. Go with the impulse, the arbitrary choice, see if you can make it work with your Juliet, her story. Be bold, kiss your Romeo, and then possibly make your way back to the more conventional, scripted "not tonight."

Writers often will use the tool of an arbitrary choice to develop a richness in their characters. In *The Pawnbroker*, a film about a Jewish shop owner who had previously been in a Nazi concentration camp, there is a particular kind of behavior and emotion, so that when gunmen enter his shop to rob him, he doesn't react as another pawnbroker might and give in, fearful for his life. This pawnbroker resists them, under the threat of death, with no regard for his own life. The logic is that because of his past horror of surviving the Holocaust, this pawnbroker has very little care any more, he's numb.

From my ancestors: Medea, at the beginning of the play, has the simple logic of a loving mother to her children. We see this fully at every turn. Her logic is love and its sweet demonstration toward her children. But then the tragic threat of losing her husband and her children to another woman forces her into an emotional logic which springs from this same love, but becomes totally opposite, totally arbitrary: In an insane, jealous rage, she murders her own children to prevent them from going with their evil father and new stepmother. Her apparent logic of sweetness and love splinters into bloody violence and death. So as actors you can use the same mechanism, the arbitrary choice, to create a new logic, something perhaps the writer didn't give you. You're not *changing* the writing, of course—but choosing something deeper that ends up revealing more about a character than would the conventional choice. (For further discussion of arbitrary choices, see the chapter, **"Arbitrary Choices."**)

19. MOMENT TO MOMENT, PART 1: BELIEF

Flexibility is to respond to the moment, not through any preconceived ideas—but directly, immediately. Immediacy is flexibility. You look to the situation, you become aware of the situation, you are sensitive to the situation— and then you act. The action comes through the encounter of the situation and you, not from a preconceived thought.

—Rajneesh (Osho), Indian
mystic and philosopher

Did you ever sit through a movie or play and have that depressing realization that you don't believe a single thing going on—nothing makes any sense, you don't believe the two stars are attracted to each other, no one is really listening to each other, and storylines lead nowhere? Suddenly your mind is busy with the notion of just walking out of the theatre, before another minute of your life is wasted. For me, unfortunately, this happens too often.

Belief is crucial for a successful movie or play—but before it happens in the audience, it must happen for you the actor. In your performance, do you believe what is occurring for you, moment to moment? I often refer to it as "tracking"—following a clear track of what is going on in the scene. So don't jump the track. When executing a behavior or action, follow it through. If the actor has chosen that the character is drunk, does he stay in line with the appropriate behavior, or does the actor suddenly drop the drunken state halfway through the scene? If you're a witness in a courtroom scene, listen to the question being asked, and answer as if you were really coming up with it right then, not as if you were reading off a page. You have to convince the jury you were not coached. Part of how you do that is of course simply to listen, to receive the information for the first time. It seems so easy—this concept of listening. It's so crucial to the art of acting, and yet it is one of the most frequent problems I see: Actors don't quite really listen to each other. You must be open and receptive, and *really hear what your partner is saying.* Let it land, and I mean "land" like those Apollo missions to the moon—those vehicles left their footprints in the sand up there, and those prints are still there. Did the line you just heard from your acting partner leave an imprint on you? It has to hit you as if for the first time. You know it's coming, but you can't anticipate the line, nor how it will affect you *until you hear it*—you have to truly discover the scene, or life itself, by listening and responding moment to moment.

That's a kind of tracking—the basic idea that the character doesn't always know what to say, and has to formulate a specific answer before speaking. When playing lovers, are the two actors really creating an intimacy with each other, or is there a guardedness between them, a physical shyness, or a bored kind of disinterest covered by pretended passion, making the audience conscious of the fact that these are just two actors and not real lovers? So actors, get to it, and passionately connect with and track the love for each other.

So the actors must believe in what's going on. The more you believe, the more you experience, and the more you experience, the more you believe—and so it goes. This is the same in life as it is in acting—the more you believe in what you're doing, the more expansive you become and the greater experience you will have. Say you're acting with your partner who's playing your husband, but you've never been married and when you do wed, it certainly won't be to this guy you're working with. Touch his face lightly. Find some feeling of intimacy in that touch. There will be something—the actor looks at you tenderly, he now lightly brushes the hair out of your face. Here's the real start of your relationship. Here's the beginning of your experience. So belief and experience feed off each other and lead to moment-to-moment work.

I will sometimes refer to "the delicatessen owner." The deli owner is the blue-collar, common-sense guy in the audience who quite correctly refers what he is seeing on stage, TV or film to the experiences of his own life, to see if this performance seems real to him. This guy doesn't know about acting. He may not know about abstract painting or atonal music, but he knows about love and sex and behavior with his wife, Bessie. If the deli owner sees two lovers on stage, behaving stiffly, without any real passion, constantly covering themselves to make sure they aren't exposing too much flesh, he might lean to his wife and whisper, "Bessie, darling, it wasn't like that when we were first in love!" You're dead as an actor when that happens.

If you're reading this and thinking this is a problem for beginning actors—you're wrong. The issue of moment-to-moment belief and experience is not just an elementary acting problem. I'd say that much of my work as a teacher even with highly professional actors has to do with this kind of work. It often happens that the working professional actor goes on a certain creative autopilot—they're a regular on a series, or they book frequent work, and it all somehow becomes a routine. Bit by bit, they start to disassociate themselves from the real communication occurring in their scenes. They don't really respond to what other actors are doing, so when one actor feeds the other a moment, our autopilot actor doesn't quite respond to it, not *really*—he just says the next line. This kind of disconnected communication is like a virus—when you let one moment like this go by, it gets in your system, multiplies, and takes over the acting. The belief isn't quite there, and then the real participation, moment to moment, which is the very lifeblood of acting, dissipates rapidly. For a professional who is still hired a lot and sometimes highly paid, cynicism sets in—the actor is applauded or paid well when they're really "phoning it in" mechanically instead of truly discovering the communication moment-to-moment.

An actor has to maintain a certain wild innocence—about his acting, about *the script:* An actor reads the script, so of course he knows what's going to happen in this story. But through fully realized moment-to-moment work, he discovers these events anew and experiences it all as though for the first time, and takes us with him in that discovery. That's acting, man. That's what I mean by innocence. Some directors are even known for withholding the later parts of the script from the actor, thus enforcing this innocence.

So ask yourself again—are you really responding to the situation step by step as a down-to-earth person would, reacting simply to each step, moment-to-moment, not anticipating, not jumping ahead to the results of the scene? Concentrate on the moment you are in—don't look ahead. The connection to your partner is a very important element here. Be like the sharp tennis player who is ready, alive and attuned to whatever his opponent sends him—the lob, the hard smash, the clever spin. This is in a way a state of listening—really perceiving what your partner sends your way. If you've ever seen a bird dog "tracking" his prey, he never loses sight, sound, smell of his prey for an instant. He is alert to whatever his prey does. And he responds to it. So when you study the concept of moment-to-moment, you're really studying the beat of life itself. In life, hopefully, you live moment to moment, believing as you go. Maybe the study of acting can *improve* your life—this attention to moment-to-moment belief can help you avoid an automatic, mechanical way of living and of acting. The concept of really listening and responding to people can lead you away from cynicism and open you to experience a fuller life, as well as being a more expressive artist.

20. MOMENT TO MOMENT, PART 2: ALTERNATIVES

To be or not to be? That is the question....

Most interpret this line in simple terms as Hamlet's decision to live or to die. I see it a bit differently: I believe he means to be—to be a person of action, a person of quality, and to act as such a person would—or not to be— simply to melt away, both physically and spiritually. There's more to it than just living or dying. What does it mean to live? What does living require of a prince, of anyone? That's what Hamlet is asking.

Meanwhile, over in *Romeo and Juliet,* Shakespeare, as he often does, invites us to deal quite directly with alternatives: He makes Juliet struggle in her monologue, desperately trying to decide whether to take the potion that will make her appear to be dead for a period of time, then wake up in the tomb where they will bury her, where she can again meet up with her lover. Paraphrasing her words: *Maybe the potion will poison me! Or I'll wake too early and the bones of my ancestors may come alive and scare the hell out of me. Oh, but if I don't take it I may never be with my love, Romeo.* Choices. Alternatives. Agony. Life! But most actresses are not engaged in that desperate decision—after all it's a very famous play and a very famous monologue and everyone out there knows she's going to take the potion.... Ah, but there's the rub.

Back to *A Streetcar Named Desire*: A moment occurs during that dinner scene I talked about earlier, where Blanche calls Stanley a Polack. There is a pause. Stanley thinks for a moment what his answer to this might be, before he impulsively smashes his dishes and food onto the floor. He has in the moment made this brutal choice. He has many possible choices before he comes up with his answer: Hit Blanche. Hit Stella. Hit both of them. Leave the table. Pack up and move out. Lecture them both about the pitfalls of this kind of prejudice. But he decides to smash his dishes, and that's what makes him Stanley. But what does he go through? What thoughts, what emotions, what possibilities does he consider before he determines what he will do? What alternatives? These possibilities are the subtext of his life before he impulsively smashes the dishes. But too often, the actor playing Stanley is not considering what could happen in this moment—and I say that process of considering what to do in this moment is as important as the action he takes.

What to do? Which way to go? Should I marry her, or no? I like her family. Well, not altogether. Not really.

Definitely not her mother. I should get out of the relationship. It's going nowhere fast. So drop it! No, no, no. Don't drop it. After all, I love her so.... Then, at the wedding ceremony, the groom must ultimately decide. *Do I go ahead with this or not?* Often he doesn't know until the last second, and then he's been known to walk out, and the same with the bride, as in movies like *The Graduate* or *Runaway Bride.* Or like that story in the news a way back about that girl who was on her way to get married, but she'd also bought a bus ticket that was in her purse. And she chose the ticket—blew off the wedding and disappeared, until they found her several days later. I love that image—all dressed for the wedding, but a bus ticket is in her purse. I wish more actors had this metaphorical bus ticket with them when they act.

Life. The weighing of possibilities. There are good points in choosing a way to go, and yet there are bad ones as well. So what to do? This is the very beat of life. In our daily lives we are constantly in the midst of deciding. Should we go to work or stay home because we don't feel well? Is it really that we don't feel well enough to work, or are we faking this malady, or maybe just emphasizing it a bit, to convince ourselves and others that bedrest is what we need? Maybe we get dressed and ready to go, but then, at the last second, just as we open the door, we decide to stay home.

Whether I'm watching a scene in class or a professional production, there's something very simple that I look for: *Is this a real person I'm looking at—someone who is alive to the moment, openly and innocently responding and deciding what to do as he goes?* Or, conversely, is this an actor—someone who only has in mind a very specific line and action that the author has written, and is waiting to deliver that line and action—and only that—when cued by that other line that the author has written, being said by another actor, who is waiting for his cue, on and on in an uneventful, unsuspenseful, unsurprising way? Without this exploration of alternatives, I believe the result is a static, boring kind of acting. A predictable kind of acting. It is this predictability that bores me. When an actor struggles between alternatives, then makes his choice, it gives both him and the audience a sense of surprise.

Recently I saw in class a scene from *Fatal Attraction,* where the husband confesses to his wife that he had an affair. The scene was well played, emotional, real—but predictable. I asked the actor a simple question: "What if your wife would have responded differently? What if she had said, *That's okay. I knew it anyway. I'm cool. It happens.*" The actor was stumped. Why was he stumped? It wasn't the response he had rehearsed. It wasn't in the script. And yet it is a possible response, probably the one he dreams, against the odds, that she will have.

Othello. Shakespeare. Alternatives. Should I kill Desdemona or no? *Yet I'll not shed her blood, nor scar that whiter skin of hers than snow, and smooth as monumental alabaster, yet she must die, else she'll betray more men.* Choices, possibilities. When you are standing next to Desdemona and you are deciding which alternative to follow—to kill her or to love her—you must fully believe in both. Actors too often believe only in the road the author has laid out. They must believe in all the roads. As Frost wrote, *Two roads diverged in a wood, and I—I took the one less traveled by, and that has made all the difference.* Othello: *To kill or to love?* Each choice must be real and absolutely possible until you finally decide. This is not a drill. It's not an exercise. It's something that should be part of your performance. *God, I love her. How can I even dream of killing her? But the bitch did it with Cassio. Death. No, I love her....* Each alternative should be explored as deeply as the one the author has written, and each should almost happen until at the last second you decide. *Kill her.*

With regard to all the tools discussed on this Checklist, know that your understanding of the circumstances of the play, your inherent belief in the situation, the responses between you and your acting partners, and your imagination can all come into play and be sufficient so that you do not necessarily need to kill yourself nailing every single item in every single scene you play. Don't get academic—no five-page papers, please. This should not be intellectual work. Doing a great scene does not mean that you can identify all 20 items and how they specifically affected you. This checklist exists to serve you, not the other way around. It could be that just really nailing the physical state will inform the entire scene and your performance will take off just using that. Strasberg said, "If you don't have a headache, don't take an aspirin." All the techniques of acting are to be used only when needed.

A REVIEW OF THE CHECKLIST

1. What is the event? What's going on in this scene? Not the theme. Just what's going on. Have I experienced anything like that? Yeah. And how did I behave? Some ideas there. Okay.

2. Evaluation. Am I on fire? Are the choices hot enough, alive? This scene is loaded. The stakes are high. Am I ready for that, or do I need to assume the position? Okay.

3. Behavior. What am I doing physically in this scene? I can't allow myself just to sit here and say lines. What else can I do to be more alive? Push-ups? Clean the room? Put on makeup? Okay.

4. Physical/Emotional State. Am I drunk? Enough? Do I feel sexy? Am I drugged, in pain? Or am I supposed to be feeling great? Just had a good food, feeling exhilarated? Am I really nailing this? And is the state consistent throughout the scene? Is it cold the entire time? Or do I warm up during the scene? How do my emotions vary in the scene? I've got to figure that out specifically. Okay.

5. What happened before the scene? Did I just finish the New York Marathon? Did I just get fired? Is it raining outside? So am I wet? Out of breath from the stairs? And how does that change now that the scene has begun? Am I tracking that clearly and logically? Okay.

6. Creative Hiding. Can I play part of the scene into the tablecloth? Weep into it? Play with my hat as I woo her? Or play the sunset instead of her eyes? Can I be freer through fiddling with the scarf? Okay.

7. **Be a person.** Am I like an actor on a stage or am I a person? My character is a person. Is my behavior coming from the real life of the character? Am I just trying to be emotional, or am I a person trying to control their emotions, as on the six-o'clock news? Okay.

8. **Inner and Outer Life "The Cover."** Play the clown for her and pretend the pain inside is nothing? Or play the pain more and less charm? Get more personal and specific with inner turmoil? I know I'll lose her—feel that? Or play more the social, easy behavior and attitude and let the inner pop out later, surprise myself and them? I need to ensure I'm not "playing the cover" without anything cooking underneath. Okay.

9. **Who's the author?** Who wrote this? Woody Allen? Bertolt Brecht? Tennessee Williams? What is this author after? What is his or her specific point of view on life? What is her style? What is his sense of humor? What other works are there by the author? Have I read them for clues? Okay.

10. **Improvisation.** I'll pretend I'm going to marry Ophelia, and we'll improvise my proposal and see where that takes us. Shakespeare's language is tough—let me say it in my own words for a while, then get back to the Bard. Let's improvise the first night of our honeymoon, see what that does for the scene. Or just be silent for a while, let the scene be within us. Loose and easy, don't push for the scene. Okay.

11. **Humor.** Am I using humor? People use humor all the time to help deal with hardship—am I doing that? Is it too much to suddenly act like Noel Coward, as Brando did at the end of *Last Tango in Paris?* Cover that pain

with a put-on, humorous, English accent? Joking with her? Yeah, that can work. All the great performances have humor, they have charm, they have irony. Okay.

12. **Trust.** Do I believe in my choices? Am I having fun? Am I confident in what I'm doing? I know it will be there, I will *make* it be there. I've got my choices. I understand this guy. Let's go. Okay.

13. **Being Personal.** Am I personally *involved* in this scene? Am I telling the right story? Being personal doesn't mean I decide the character is from my home town. This needs to cost me something: My emotional involvement. My blood, sweat, and tears, while I serve the story. Okay.

14. **Pathology.** How sick is this character? How compulsive? Am I giving in to the violence? I have some seed of this in my life. Use it. Expand on it. Remember, he will do anything to possess her. Okay.

15. **Objectives.** The character wants to be king, don't deny it. Do I want it enough? I know what it means to want something. Go for it. Remember, at any cost he wants to seduce her, so am I doing all I can to get her? Caution is not my friend. Okay.

16. **Specifics.** Is this my Hamlet, personal and specific? Do I have the father? Is he real to me? The image of my mother in bed with my uncle—do I have that? It's late at night. Do I have the specific feeling of late at night; not tired, but hyper? The choice of Hamlet's angry explosion, do I have that nailed? Really? Okay.

17. **Use of Objects.** Am I using physical objects to connect myself with this environment? Maybe some of my own personal objects will make me more comfortable. Or how about one that has more emotional value for me? Yeah, let me use one of those. Any inner objects I can think of that will help me connect with moments in the scene? Okay.

18. **Arbitrary Choices:** Kazan says, "Character is revealed through contradiction." What inner struggle is my character going through that might be revealed through an arbitrary choice? Some kind of illogical choice that actually fits the truth of this guy? Okay.

19. **Moment to moment: Belief.** Can this scene be tracked? Am I responding to things moment to moment? Am I really listening, taking the time to respond as a person would? Am I discovering each moment as it happens? The more I experience, the more I'll believe, and the more I believe, the more I'll experience. Okay.

20. **Moment to moment: Alternatives.** The script says my character leaves his wife. But have I explored the opposite? That he stays? Maybe he tries to stay, but at the last second he can't. Real people go through tough decision making before choosing the way to go. So as an actor, I need to go through that process, even though the final action has been determined by the author. I have to participate in the process. That needs to be part of my performance. Okay.

Class Exercises

The notion of acting class exercises often conjures up some pretty tiresome images—akin to what the girl talked about in *A Chorus Line*—pretending to be a table, be a sports car, or an ice-cream cone. As I've already mentioned, my approach as a teacher is based in my experience as a director, and I almost never have time for exercises as a director. That being said, below are some I believe to be down-to-earth, common-sense, and can help the actor solve certain issues. These should be done only as needed, and then what you get—put it to use in your next scene. Please understand: These exercises are to be done and supervised by a trained teacher, not done alone by the actor.

1. Song and Dance Exercise
2. Picture Exercise
3. Creating an Environment
4. Personal Monologue
5. Audition Exercise
6. Improvisation Exercise
7. Relaxation Exercise
8. Shoot Exercise

1. OPEN UP—THE SONG AND DANCE EXERCISE

This exercise has two parts. First, the actor stands in front of the class and sings, trying to keep his body relaxed and still. He puts concentration on his feelings, his impulses, and tries to experience them and release them. At first his emotional response may be slight, but as the actor becomes more relaxed, I want him to coax those small impulses, try to encourage them. Usually there are specific points of physical tension that serve to hold your impulses, your emotions in check. So part of the exercise is to become aware of this tension, where it resides, and how to release it, allowing the inner feelings to come out. Don't dissipate these feelings with fidgeting, spasms, nervous rocking or any talk. When the actor is inhibited from extraneous movement in this exercise, the emotions often become much more available. With one actress I found that as she was singing, she was holding her thumb and finger together, tightly. Very tightly. As soon as I saw that and made her release the tension there, she started crying. The same occurred with an actor who kept raising his eyebrows. I just took my hand and tried to loosen that area—bang. Emotion. So it's about trying to locate that tension. I try to be somewhat gentle with the actor, a little humorous—they're often nervous about standing there in front of the class, so I try to get them to relax and have a sense of humor about it.

In the second part of the exercise, the actor is instructed to carry out specific movements and rhythms of various kinds, like jazz, marching, jumping, and to sing out fully. The effort is intended to release the voice and body to a freer expressiveness. So when the emotions haven't been tapped during the first part of the exercise, sometimes the physical activity of the second will help loosen them up.

With this exercise, open your voice. Get in touch with any mild sensation that can lead you further to a strong emotional response. Allow the emotional connection. Experience freedom of rhythm and movement, connect with what is happening, and deal with tension, attitudes, and defenses that might interfere with your emotional responsiveness. This exercise is very good for close-ups, by the way—it can develop the ability for a strong emotional response without any jerky movements, keeping yourself in the frame. The actor is capable of experiencing anything, but in some cases needs to be trained to get out of his or her own way and allow the experience to happen. (For further discussion of the song and dance exercise, see the chapter, **"Exposing the Secret."**)

2. DETAILS, BABY—THE PICTURE EXERCISE

Find a painting or a photograph of a character: let's say one of artist Toulouse-Lautrec's ladies. Create the exact physical pose the character has in the picture, the exact makeup and costume—this will enhance the reality, and hence your own belief. Aim to create the exact pose, the character's attitude, the inner emotional life, the outer physical life, the full, real sense of the person in the picture. Really be the character. It's a matter of getting so into the picture or painting that you are almost possessed by it.

Once you nail the pose and that inner and outer life, then the exercise can be expanded by adding movement or behavior, by saying a few sentences or a poem or a monologue, all of which emanate from the character you've created based on the photograph. This work on behavior must come from the picture. It's as if you couldn't do what you are doing without the picture having informed that choice. If you speak, don't try just to be clever, don't come up with lines that you think explain the biography of the character. Just try to be true to this person. If, as you do the exercise, your work on the character weakens, go back into the pose of the picture— get reconnected, get re-involved.

As the actor connects with the picture and begins to take on the characteristics of the person portrayed, a transformation occurs into a specific character. This is very detailed work, done by the actor outside class in preparation for the exercise. You must pay strict attention to the nth degree of the pose, the emotional attitude, and the inner life of the person in the picture— the hand gesture, the position of the shoulder. Where is the character looking? In what manner? What is he or she thinking? Now you must execute physically and emotionally what you see, and through this execution you involve yourself in the creation of the character. Through this exercise, the actor gains a power, clarity, and definition of the character that he would not otherwise have. Exact physical duplication and a real investigation of the emotional life are both keys to fulfilling the exercise.

In terms of selecting a photograph, it is best not to choose an actor or model or some other celebrity—because their personalities can be well-known, the exercise then becomes one of mimicry. Instead, find a connection with just a real person. Find a butcher. Find a housewife. The possibilities are endless. It's about you and that photograph. A full-body shot is generally better than a close-up, because you can see the clothes, the posture, and you can better assess the behavior you need to create. It's best if you have an emotional response or connection to the picture that will motivate and propel you. Don't cop out by choosing a picture of someone who happens to wear the clothes you already have in your closet. Find someone you have to reach for, who challenges you. Don't use a mirror to prepare, other than maybe to check the pose a few times. Instead, try to rely on your sense of observation and perception to duplicate the posture and the attitude. As you prepare the exercise, see if you can take the character out—go ahead and take him or her out to the grocery market and feel the real life there, interact with real people. Unless, of course, your character is from another century or has a strange costume or something that will get you in trouble with the police. Although that might be interesting, too!

An actress who was in the original *Roots* was in class with me when she was offered a role in the sequel, which would have required her to play someone much older than she was. She was panicked that she couldn't pull off playing the older age, and was ready to turn down the part. I had her bring in a picture exercise of an older woman—she brought in a picture of her aunt. She really nailed the exercise, and as a result her own belief was enhanced and she ended up booking the part in the sequel.

The American actor is accused of not being as good as the British in creating a character. Bullshit. Dustin Hoffman as a 100-year-old Indian in *Little Big Man*. Brando as *The Godfather*. Walter Huston in *Treasure of the Sierra Madre*. Streep in *Sophie's Choice*. Kathy Bates in *Misery*. Gloria Swanson in *Sunset Boulevard*. So there is a history of great character work by American actors, and this exercise helps develop the tools that will continue that tradition.

3. BE THERE FOR THE PAYOFF—CREATING AN ENVIRONMENT

You're at home, working on your stamp collection, your painting, your writing work. You're very involved. You look at your watch—you've been doing this for an hour and a half, absorbed, lost in the activity. This is what is possible in your acting work: really creating a place and your involvement in an activity.

The environmental exercise helps the actor create a place and this involvement: bedroom, office, kitchen, workroom, or whatever environment the actor assigns. The exercise is used to make those places more specific and personal by adding the actor's own hairbrush, or an actress's makeup on her own dressing table, or more emotionally charged objects such as family photos, an heirloom brooch, a personal letter, etc. The actor assembles furniture and props to create a place, specific and believable, so that the environment is vital in centering the actor in a reality.

The purpose of the exercise in the end is to get the actor *involved*, living and functioning as a person in a room, rather than an actor on a stage. A couple of boxes and a chair won't do the job. You really have to invest in creating your space with your objects. Don't just bring three books and a bedspread. Really create your own space. Then discover some involving activity that interests the hell out of you, a behavior that engages your concentration, your creativity—not something banal. I'm not wild about painting one's nails while text messaging. Reading *People* magazine? Banned. I've seen a few new male actors in class choose some masturbation ritual. Now, as Victor Borge said, "Unless of course you absolutely *have* to...," I'd rather you didn't, as it seems geared more toward showing off a certain bravado than about the exercise itself. Cooking? Okay, if you're good, and if you take care and are really involved. Definitely not stapling headshots. You must have something you like to do that uses the creative part of your mind, right? Something that really involves you. You've got these kinds of activities—Come on!

Over the years, I have added a wrinkle to the environmental exercise. The actor has a task and a life in the space, but now as the actor becomes fully absorbed and relaxed and at ease, a crisis occurs: the phone rings with news that someone dear has been hurt in an accident; a letter arrives from a lover breaking off the relationship; you find your spouse's diary and discover a terrible secret; a person comes to deliver you a court summons. The actor, absorbed by his behavior, relaxed and at ease in the space, has not anticipated the crisis and responds to it more naturally, more deeply. The idea here is not to show off your writing skills, creating a minutes-long telephone call of epic tragic proportions. The class need not even know what the crisis is. With your involved activity as the foundation, the simple point of the crisis is to discover your response to it. It needs to hit you. Don't spend time away from class heavily preparing the crisis and your response. Just pick something hot, or you can even have in mind two or three possible crises, have the idea of what they might be before you go, but then really let it happen right there during the exercise. As you do the exercise, you can pick the one that seems hottest at the moment. Receive the crisis quickly and respond to it (remember to use the tools of reflective delay and the "six o'clock news" concept). Does your behavior change? How so? How is your concentration on the activity you've been doing in the exercise altered by the crisis? Do you try to return to the activity, but you can't? Discover the answers as you do this exercise. Don't just receive the bad news, sit down, and cry. Respond behaviorally, using your environment to help you.

4. A KEY TO YOU—THE PERSONAL MONOLOGUE

You need to be personal in your work always. Towards that result, the personal monologue is a powerful tool. You write a piece, not being concerned about whether it's a play or not, just something you feel strongly about. It could be about your life directly: your struggle as an immigrant child trying to connect with a new country; or your struggle to come to grips with a father who has never expressed his love. One recent monologue was about the actor's struggle to become a person and not just a "spoiled rich kid." Another actor wrote about his struggle with his attitude toward reading for a part, and the doubting voice within him that prevented positive results. So you take one of these personal situations and write or improvise the monologue in the class, connecting very intimately with the experience you're covering. It's not necessary for the monologue to be true, by the way. An actress in class did one where she talked about how she had been diagnosed with terminal cancer—by the end of the monologue the whole class was in tears, and then it turned out she made the thing up. (Actors sometimes can be downright ornery.)

The personal monologue eggs you on to become more vulnerable. It's about your life, your feelings, your emotions. Naked personal involvement. An evocative experience that springs from you spontaneously and emotionally. It reveals the depth of emotion, the power of your own experience. You can take this powerful experience to any play or film you work on by applying the same kind of immediacy and passion that you had in the personal monologue.

The personal monologue should be a process. It should affect you as an actor and possibly as a person. You should be trying to work something out in the personal monologue—it should be about something, and you should learn something from doing it. Be careful not just to sit in a chair and bemoan how awful your childhood was. Get creative. An actor once did a personal monologue about why he didn't work in the industry more. I told him he should ask the class, "Why don't I work more?" The answers from the class were frank and direct, and led the actor to look at real issues about himself that opened his eyes. I once wrote a personal monologue for an actress, in which she acted out excerpts from various roles that I thought she could play. Not only did she create a fabulous character for each role, but she let the performance of each of those monologues affect her as she went from one to another, finally culminating in a very personal statement of her doubts about ever achieving these roles. Very dangerous for her. Risky. It was her best work ever as an actress.

As Hamlet, your job as the actor is not to be a professional puppet, echoing Shakespeare's words through his ventriloquist character. You are an artist creating on-the-spot behavior, experiences, and dialogue that should seem as if you yourself had authored it, even though it's Shakespeare's. The personal monologue makes it clear to you that your personal story can be emotional and passionate, and so allows you to believe in your power as an actor to make even Shakespeare personal. (For a further discussion of the Personal Monologue, see the chapter, **"Personal Confidence."**)

5. GO FOR IT, IT'S YOURS—THE AUDITION EXERCISE

In an audition exercise, we set up a casting office on stage, and we'll have classmates play a casting person and/or a director, and the actor will come in and do whatever he or she actually does at an audition. The actor can bring "sides" from an audition he or she already had, or the material may be chosen for them. This is a very revealing exercise. Because aside from the acting part of it, you'll often spot physical mannerisms, or an attitude that the actor brings into the audition that is not productive, no matter how good the acting is. But of course, you can also see what the actor does with regard to the choices about character and script. As a teacher, I can count on the fact that the Audition Exercise will yield about three times the number of questions from the class as scenes—because of course, everyone wants to be better at booking work. So here are my thoughts on this for now, with more to come in the Administration section as well:

First off, there are no readings, only actings. When auditioning, you must act the part, not read it. The casting people want to see that you can do the part, and you must reveal to them your acting ability and your rightness for this role. You're telling them, "Relax—I can do it." And part of the equation is creating a sense that there's even more to come if they give you the role. So yes, you nail the acting, *and* make them feel as if there is more discovery ahead.

Sometimes you can be more effective by creating a place in which to play the scene by moving the furniture in the casting office where possible. In other words, take possession of the space—but be quick about it. They're on a schedule. Many readings these days are occurring for camera—they're recording your audition to show the director later on. You may have to stand on a mark or sit in a particular chair. No problem. They may want you to play directly to the camera lens, or to the person in the room next to the camera. No problem. You're a professional, right? So do what they ask. *I can play* The Iceman Cometh *in a chair. I can do Romeo into a lens. I can be emotional while moving or not moving.* You have to stay relaxed and as flexible as you can about it. It probably won't come down to movement, anyhow. It's going to come down to acting: Discern what is happening in the scene in the simplest sense, nail who the character is, make an acting choice which is alive for you, some choice that fires you, keep it simple—and go for it.

My advice is always to hold the script, even if you know the lines. If you present a memorized audition they'll see you in terms of a "finished performance," and you're not there yet. Again, let them think there's more to come. The idea behind holding the script for lines is "Pay me and I'll learn them." Really commit to your acting partner, even if it's a casting person who doesn't give much. Some actors say after a reading, "I couldn't do anything. The person I was reading with was a zombie." This defense does not hold up in court. The professional actor can play passionately to a door. The professional actress can be a seductive Miss Julie to a broom. And sometimes you might prefer the broom! If you finish a reading and feel that you didn't do what you wanted, go ahead—ask to do it one more time. Even if you're in your car on the way home. Turn around. Go back. But if you do, and they let you read again, you'd better be damned good!

I think actors freak out about auditions because they literally think they're going to die. It's a wild thought, but it's as if they're reminded of some time in the distant ancient past when they had to plead their case before an austere magistrate who—if they failed to convince him— took their house, their family, their life. With or without this ancient scenario, actors feel the terror of the test. Therefore, know an audition is going for a job, a part, a stepping stone in your career, not life and death. Robert DeNiro did a talk at Paramount once, and responding to a question about auditions, said, "Look, you go in, you read, you do the best you can, you go home. You're probably not going to get the job, anyway." There's a certain relaxedness that I like about that. It is only one part, there will be many more.

I often hear actors tell me that they feel the part they're reading for is too small, the material too stupid, that for whatever reason they really don't want the part. If that is the case—don't go. Really. Don't do yourself and the producers an injustice by reading for a part you don't really want. Be willing to be honest with yourself about the material and the role, and communicate with your agents. If you're not into the part, don't read for it. Or change your mind about it, and go in with some enthusiasm, knowing full well that these opportunities, and your response to them, are a part of your life as an actor. And you must work professionally. There are no actors, as there are other artists, such as painters and composers, who are discovered after they are dead.

Sometimes you'll encounter a situation, it may be within an audition setting, or it may be a separate "general" meeting, where you simply have to be conversational with the director or writer. Don't be this person:

> *"Well, the last thing I did was this project, The Werewolf Eats Gidget, it was really small, I mean, like I shot a day on it. But I'm feeling more confident. In class they're talking to me a lot about my confidence. My therapist is helping, too. And it's working, because I'm feeling better, even though I still hate LA. Except for the food. I'm a bit, I know, distracted...I just broke up with my guy....*

Do not talk about your last acting job, the art of acting, or your life as an actor. Talk about the paintings in the room, last Sunday's football game, hot fashion items, or other current matters that interest you. Your job here is just to be *a person*. Be charming. Be confident. Let them know you see them as individuals, and let them see where you are coming from. If you have a passion for politics or painting or music, let them know. And ask about them—always good to be more interested in them than you're interested in you. Remember, they are looking for someone. They need to fill a role. What they actually want is to resolve a situation: an uncast part. You could be their answer.

By the way, if you are not their answer, either from a reading or interview, fine. Just go about your business. Get in your car and go. Have lunch. Clean the house, plant flowers, read a book, wrestle with a Turk, or rehearse a scene for class. Do not dwell on the possible reasons as to why and wherefore you didn't get the part. Instead, write a nice letter. The letter should be along the lines of what a pleasure it was to meet them, thanks for the opportunity, if anything ever comes up, etc. Many actors have gotten work based on a good follow-up letter after having been turned down for a part.

And regarding "feedback": it is often unclear, inaccurate, unusable. No matter what the feedback is, the truth of the matter is you do not know what was said by whom to whom regarding your audition. It's unknowable. It's presented as "fact," but you simply do not know unless the director is speaking to you personally. I once turned down an actor for a part because I felt he had too much of a streetwise quality. The agent passed along to him that I thought he was "too sleazy." This actor was a friend of mine, and it affected the relationship for years. So don't listen to feedback. Don't doubt your own existence and your reasons for being an actor. Have dignity, work on yourself, study, and it will come. Persist. Persist. Persist.

6. DON'T GET CLEVER—THE IMPROVISATION EXERCISE

Just as two chemicals react when mixed with each other, so do two people—but contrary to what you may think, *words are not the catalyst.* What is happening between people, the emotional interchange, the subtext—this is what drives a story. In teaching, I use an improvisation exercise as a tool to drive home this lesson. In addition to the various ways to use improvisation as discussed above, which can be considered exercises in their own right, this specific Improvisation Exercise is used to help develop the actor's impulses and ability to discover each moment anew, fresh, using their imagination, without preconception or roadmap or censorship.

The idea is that I'll get at least two actors to come up on stage. I may give a circumstance to both, or just to one of the actors. But often what I like to do is set up improvisations where very little or no information is given. Maybe I'll just whisper to one of the actors: *You need to break up with him.* So what's going on? With either a few words from me or none, the actors are forced to relate to each other, trying to discover the answer from their partner. *Why is she being cold to me? What's going on with her today?* The actors have to search, really look for new, honest answers—rather than those that might have been glibly available had I told them a bunch of circumstances for the improvisation, or where I wanted it to go. They can't rely on Stanislavski's aforementioned "muscle of the tongue"—the actor's facility with language or words used as a substitute for honest emotions and behavior. I don't want them to write a clever story with funny lines. The desired result is for a spontaneous moment-to-moment experience for the actors, which leads to deeper emotion, behavior, and communication with their partners—and surprises. The power of the exercise is huge in getting the actors not to think, but to be caught off-guard, and so experience more and find the real truth of their personal responses. It's a kind of risky fun, and often humorous—but hopefully not just because of clever lines, but through human interaction.

7. RELAXATION EXERCISE

The strings on the violin or piano—too tight? Snap. Shrill. Too loose? No sound, bland. Try playing a violin with strings made of cooked spaghetti. No go. A balance is needed between relaxation and tension. Relaxation is necessary for the easy flow of energy, emotion, and physical activity from the actor. Excessive tension can stop this flow for sure, but I believe a performer also needs a bit of that metaphorical string tension in order to be at his or her best.

Every so often in class, when I have a student whose tension has become an obstacle to their expressiveness, I will do a relaxation exercise. In this exercise, the actor sits in a chair and simply tries to fall asleep. The attention of the actor is directed toward a specific body part where tension exists. Once the actor spots the area of tension, often relaxation will quickly occur. Common areas are around the mouth, back of the neck, lower back, and at the temples. I coax him to either gently move these parts to relieve the tension, or lightly massage the areas such as the tiny muscles around the mouth, or gently move and roll the head to relieve tension in the neck. In this simple way, relief from tension can happen. This is best done with a teacher present, but certainly simply trying to fall asleep in a chair can be done as relaxation before doing a scene in class or professionally.

In dealing with tension and relaxation, one must be able to differentiate between a negative kind of nervousness (fearful, introverted, shaky) and a positive excitement (stimulated, stirred, induced to action). Nervousness can be your enemy, can hold you back, interfere with your creative intensity. Excitement can be a friend, helpful if used properly, making you more alive and expressive.

So in working on relaxation, you must be careful not to water down your intensity. Some actors have the misunderstanding that they should be absolutely calm, that their heartbeats should not accelerate a jot, that they should be on stage or in front of the camera just as they are reading the newspaper and having coffee on a leisurely Sunday morning. Should the actor be completely calm? Not necessarily. You only need to be relaxed to the extent that emotions, energy, and physical behavior are not impeded. If you feel the pulse racing, this may be just the excitement of acting, which is positive. But if you really are feeling impeded, that's a sign of tension, which is a negative, so that's a moment when you can try the relaxation exercise. But this should be done judiciously to balance things out. My opinion is that too much time is devoted to dealing with the so-called problem of nervousness and tension so that relaxation becomes an end in itself, often replacing intensity and excitement with dullness and lack of energy. A relaxed, no intensity, apathetic, loose-as-a-noodle actor is not your sexiest, most dangerous Richard III.

8. THE SHOOT EXERCISE

In a Shoot Exercise, the actors choose a scene in advance to perform, but they don't rehearse. They memorize the material on their own, individually. The most they do together is run the lines just before the scene goes up, maybe agree on a set plan for the stage, but that's it. They have to rely on their talent, their impulses, their ability to observe and listen and respond to their partner *in that moment*. Hopefully the freedom of a Shoot Exercise can be refreshing—the scene isn't overworked. It's not overthought. There's no guilt about whether the rehearsal process was detailed enough. The imagination flies, and the actor can feel freer to let it rip.

The idea here is that the actors should be able to apply the lessons they've been learning through rehearsed scene work to the more likely professional circumstance, particularly in film and television, which is that there may be very little or zero rehearsal before the cameras are turned on. You may ask why if the realistic professional circumstance in film and TV is little or no rehearsal, why train on all these in-depth, rehearsed and researched scenes? Because you have to learn to do the necessary work in a methodical fashion before you apply it on the fly. People will often remark to a talented artist, director, musician, or any skilled tradesperson: *How did you do that so well, and so effortlessly?* Well, through years of methodical study, apprenticeship and experience, that's how! The Shoot Exercise is there to put this acquired ability to the test.

In the theatre, of course, weeks of rehearsal is the norm, and even on film projects, the more rehearsal that occurs before filming, the better the chances are that the project will move forward efficiently. So this exercise allows the actors who have been in class a while the chance to see how their work can be applied in a zero rehearsal environment, but it's not something I recommend for newer actors in class, nor as a steady diet during your studies.

So these are the exercises I use. They are simple, and I hope clear. They are training tools, and keep in mind as I said—to be used if the actor is having a particular problem. They can be great fun. But—no headache? No aspirin necessary.

In all this work on Technique....

imagination, n., We would define imagination to be the will working on the materials of memory, not satisfied with following the order prescribed by nature, or suggested by accident, it selects the parts of different conceptions, or objects of memory, to form a whole, more pleasing, more terrible or more awful than has ever been presented in the ordinary course of nature.

Webster's Dictionary, 1904

Indicating

In acting, to indicate is to show, I repeat, *show* the audience feeling, emotion, character through external means, through gesture, through demonstration, energy, voice, without really feeling or experiencing the moment. It's a token, a symbol, an indication, the shell of the thing without internal connection or actual experience. The audience often experiences it as a presentational expression and is not fully moved by this approach. It could be that the indicating actor is skilled enough to fool the audience, but only up to a point, and he doesn't really carry the emotional power to move us, not as much as if he used his full acting instrument really to experience the story. Indicating means you are showing or pointing at something to bring the audience's attention to it. It means you are separate from your character, saying you *are* something when in fact you are *not*: "His heavy breathing and rolling of the eyes indicated to the audience that he was passionate." This is describing an actor who is not involved, not really moved, just show and tell.

So we have basically two categories of actors: the presentational actor, and the real or feeling actor. One is pretend and the other real. The feeling actor's intention is moment-to-moment experience and involvement. The event of the play or film happens to him, and he changes as a result of the experience, and in this way, he genuinely affects the audience. Through his involvement he involves the audience. The presentational actor creates effects, making the "appropriate" gestures, vocal inflections and insinuations that will elicit the "appropriate" responses from the audience. He may think he is being honest, but in fact he is not aware of the insidious theatrical habits and tricks he has accumulated over the years.

One example somewhat out of the field of acting (although everyone is acting sometimes) is a *maitre d'*. Walk into a restaurant and you might see one so full of himself, pretending to be concerned about you, carrying on with pretentious gestures and behavior, kissing the hand of your lady in a phony way, his full attention on his immaculately cut Italian jacket, showing off his Armani tie and his new haircut, coiffed perfectly with a curl hanging delicately on his sunburned forehead, as he says, "So, so good to see you again!" No, he doesn't care about seeing you or anything about you. He pretends he does, but the show is for him. The real *maitre d'* may have many similarities, but his basic intent is to care for you, to see that you are happy, and to do his job smoothly without phony promises or lies about the quality of the food. He will, in fact, steer you away from what he knows is not fresh fish on that particular day.

So the real actor is more interested in the truth of the character he's playing, and the indicator is more interested in himself, in showing off through the character he's playing. The indicator is interested in himself in art. The real is interested in the art in himself. The indicator wants to be interesting, the real to be interested. The indicator doesn't need to open his heart; the real opens his heart in order to be personally connected.

The power of a play or film is in its subtext. What is going on between the characters that isn't being said?

The indicator gives us an illustration of the play's surface, not a deep-felt expression of the true undercurrent of the moment or character. The indicator may touch the subtext, but highly underestimates its importance.

Don't be weakened by your desire to please. In performance the pressure is on, so stick to your choices. Pressure can lead to expediency, indication. Make your choice clearly and pursue it with as little compromise as possible. Of course, there are no absolutes; an actor may slip into indicating here and there, but it can't be the primary mode of operation, it can't be the basic intent of the actor. Basic intent determines the essence of an actor. All artists have to make a choice. Are you there to fool the audience with pretentious indication, or to reveal your character to them through your own heart?

Getting Personal

I've observed over the years that there is a certain breed of actor, often professionally successful, who seems generally to perform in a more theatrical style. Sometimes this particular cat has an entertaining or creative way of expressing himself, developed and honed over the years. He considers this style as very useful for professional work—it's an automatic kind of behavior, a rote way of working. I have a love for these actors, for sure, but the possible bad news is my observation that they are not as personal as I believe they can be. Because they can often be successful, this actor can present quite a challenge to a teacher trying to develop a more personal, more real, more down-to-earth approach to their work. Here's a conversation I had with such an actor, while driving a fast car rather recklessly down the freeway.

MILTON: You're a good actor, but there's something missing.

ACTOR: What is it?

A silence ensues, as Milton continues his reckless driving.

MILTON: Well, it's something to do with you as a person. This sounds funny, but it's *you* that's missing.

Long pause.

ACTOR (*panicked*): It's me, isn't it? There's something wrong with me. Right?

MILTON: Take it easy. Could you make sure that your door is locked? I don't want an actor suddenly throwing himself on the freeway at seventy miles an hour.

ACTOR: Well, fuck! *It's me that missing in my acting.* Wow. No one's ever said *that* to me, that's for sure.

MILTON: But look, you're successful, you may not want this talk.....

ACTOR: Fuck that! Don't back off of it. Let's go. We're there. This is the moment. Keep going. Can you drive a little slower?

Milton continues speeding.

MILTON: Well, you said you wanted to do *The Entertainer*....

ACTOR: Yeah, my concept is I was going to do it as the sorrowful clown.

MILTON: That's good, but the sorrowful clown can become a generality. What I want to see is *you and your personal struggle* as an actor. Your sadness. Your entertainer. Personal. The real deal.

ACTOR: The real deal. I mean, it's not like I've tried to avoid bringing the real deal. Have I...?

Pause. Milton just drives.

MILTON: Look, not every part you play should be based in a theatrical, flamboyant quality. For example, you know all about shoemakers, your father was a shoemaker from Ohio, but if I were going to do a film about a shoemaker from Ohio, you would want to play the rich count who was bringing his boots to be repaired. The count coming off his yacht to bring his elegant, flamboyant boots into the simple shop, but not the earthy shoemaker.

ACTOR: That's funny—because nobody has ever believed that I'm actually from Ohio. It's like they go off this image I give them—everyone asks, "Are you from Vienna? Paris? Venice?," some exotic place. And it's not like I correct them, do I? It's not like I say proudly, "I am from Ohio!" I have created this actor image—the count, the marquis, the baron, some old phony vaudevillian—and I'm stuck with it.

Both sit silently. The actor stares out the window into the distance.

ACTOR: Twenty years of faking, pretending. I've lost my authenticity.

MILTON: Right—that's true to a certain degree. The vaudevillian is delicious, but it isn't really you. We want you. We want your essence.

ACTOR: When Picasso does the *Guernica*, his essence is right there. We know what a Spanish peasant feels about the Fascist destruction of a Spanish town.

MILTON: And Goya said, "The soul of the painter is in every stroke."

ACTOR: I remember when we went to the museum to see that Picasso exhibit. The *Guernica* always stayed with me. It's like Picasso's personal horror is in that horse, in that woman's face. His personal feelings come through in his art. Is that what you're talking about?

MILTON: Starting to sound pretty good to me.

ACTOR: I'm getting it I think. The personal connection to a role. It's like the personal connection makes a seamless bond between the actor and the character. I can always be the flamboyant guy when I want to, but it isn't something I'm stuck with, an automatic way or a habit.

MILTON: Bingo! That's it. I couldn't have said it better myself.

ACTOR: It feels like I'm starting all over, like I have to learn to walk all over again. Watching myself.

MILTON: Well, part of what I'm doing as a teacher is to try to get the actor to see himself coming down the pike, see who he is, what he puts out there, his flaws as well as his strengths, then when needed he can change.

ACTOR: It's a little scary, to be honest.

MILTON: Don't worry, Strasberg used to say, "You were eating apple pie, so now try cherry pie. You can always go back to apple."

ACTOR: Yeah. But it's still like I'm starting over.

MILTON: Not really. You have many professional victories, no one can take that from you. This is about the future.

ACTOR: Yeah. If you don't kill us with your driving today, my next scene is going to be different. Get ready for me. The Ohio, no-bullshit me!

Observation of Life

There is a huge reservoir of creative possibilities that pass before the artist and are available as a stimulus for his work: the way people behave in a supermarket; different walks and attitudes on the boulevard; intimate reactions with family and friends; the free and open behavior of children; the bold and uncensored remarks of the elderly; the specific movement, interchange, body language, temperament, and instinctual behavior of animals. Life is a cornucopia of riches, a limitless, vital, and experiential feast for the artist to observe, draw from and so be inspired. Don't draw from theatre, movies, or other art forms alone. Draw from the theatre, and you copy; draw from life, and you originate. Be interested in life. If you are interested, then your performances and life itself will be interesting.

When you sit in a car at a red light and someone walks by, you can see who they are. If you're really observing, you can see their economics, their sexuality, their politics, their point of view—because there is a kind of life energy and music that emanates from them. Observe. Look. See. Learn to tune yourself into this station. A piano needs someone to play it, but as an actor you are both the piano and the pianist.

So study life, notice in detail the gestures of people. Look for the model of the character you are working on, find him in life: at the fruit stand, on the docks, in a luxurious department store, sleeping under a bridge. Observe your model, try out the specifics at home, then bring them to rehearsal; see what works. Observe the emotions in yourself and others. Study reactions to life's situations; often they are very different from what you think they would be. Incorporate newly-discovered truth in your work. Go to the zoo, study the animals. They have less to hide than their human counterparts. Think of your character in animal traits: tiger, monkey, rhino; let this affect your work. Allow the animal to uncover new rhythms, new movements. Talk to people on the street: police, whores, hard hats, street cleaners, garbage men, shop owners. Communicate with them, interact, observe, learn to look at details. Put them in your work. Play with children, feel their uninhibited freedom. Put it in your work. When a crisis occurs, observe yours and others' responses. At a funeral, a picnic, a ballgame, a dance recital: observe, gather information, retain the images and impressions. In the observation of life, there is the observation of yourself and the awareness and uncovering of life in yourself, including sensory experiences accumulated during a day, a year, a lifetime. You contain all that is needed within you. Put it in your work. As I was writing the book, a friend of mine who is a very talented scenic designer said he observes life all the time, every day, and that's part of what makes him a good designer. The tough part is that when you actually observe, really observe, really notice—you have to care. You can't look around you, really see what's happening, and not care about it. So this observation of life is about—sorry—developing your soul. The richer your life, the more complex, the more you are in touch with what's around you, the better artist you are going to be. So participate in the great feast of life, observe, and as you do, put it in your work.

The Study of the Arts

What do I need to know? You must know everything.
—Isaac Babel, Russian author and playwright

"I can't talk to you now.... Well, I have to stop off and listen to the rehearsal of the Shostakovich in the music hall. I gotta run. Friday night? I can't rehearse early, I'm going to an exhibition of art student paintings on the second floor. But let's rehearse later after that...."

One of the strongest attributes of the university I attended, Carnegie Mellon, was that painters, architects, sculptors, musicians, dancers and actors all studied together in one building. Each influenced the other. We would attend one another's performances and exhibitions. This was not only educational, but the influence of each art on the other was very stimulating. The fully developed actor needs knowledge, familiarity, and an understanding of all the arts. The study of life and the study of art is an ongoing, ever-developing feast of delights, possibilities and practical tools that will nurture the artist forever. In the creation of theatre and film productions, many arts participate and contribute to the final resolution.

You may find your character in a painting; music gives you an emotional response for the scene; a novel may illuminate a human quality you can apply. The arts are tied together like a family, out of the same seed, and strongly influence one another. As an actor, you need familiarity with theatre writing from Greek drama to Mamet. You need to know films past and present. The actor should be attending the opera, dance, concerts, museums, art galleries, performance pieces, as well as theatre and cinema. I was lucky because I went to university at an arts institute, but any city has museums, concerts, galleries, music rehearsals, dance recitals—avail yourself of all of it. As an actor, you are part of the family of the arts. So get to know and be intimate with your family.

Exposing The Secret

Mama's Little Darling

An actress stands before the class on an empty stage. Milton stands next to her.

MILTON: Now, why are you doing this song and dance exercise?

ACTRESS: Because you suggested it to me.

MILTON: I always love that answer. But why do *you* think we're doing it?

Milton tries to move her arms away from her torso— they're stiff, not moving freely. He continues moving various parts of her body.

ACTRESS: Well, I have a feeling that I'm probably blocking somewhere and that I'm not free.

MILTON: But you're not sure. This is more Milton's trip. Relax the jaw.

ACTRESS: Well, I have a feeling that it's going to be a real good thing for me.

MILTON: Right. You've got some secret. Tell me about it.

Milton tries to move the arms again, but they're still pretty tightly held at the shoulder. He moves her right arm out at 90-degree angle to her body. It just stays there.

ACTRESS: Well. I think I probably am a little bit prim....

MILTON: A tight-ass?

ACTRESS: I wouldn't say that....

Class laughter. Her arm is still hanging rigidly at a 90-degree angle.

MILTON: You mind letting this arm go for me?

Actress suddenly becomes aware—the arms drops relaxedly to her side.

MILTON: Okay, not a tight-ass. What was your word? Prim?

ACTRESS (*Defensively*): Yeah. What's wrong with prim?

MILTON: Getting a little hostile there, are you? Okay. Let's get to it. I've had a hard time reaching you. Today, you're going to tell me your secret. Begin. Sing.

Actress sings her song, while Milton continues to check her arms, shoulders, neck, jaw, etc., for tension.

MILTON: What did you get out of that, just now, the singing?

ACTRESS: I felt some anger. And some fear.

MILTON: And some sexuality?

ACTRESS: I missed that.

Class laughter.

MILTON: You missed it?

ACTRESS: Oh, yeah.

MILTON: Were you trained in how to look by someone?

ACTRESS: Trained in how to look?

MILTON: In other words, "Little darling, we're going to this dance, we're going to this party. I want you to smile, and I want your face in a certain way." Am I getting warm?

ACTRESS: I suppose so. My mom and grandmother—they are very proper.

MILTON: Yeah. But this is an exercise where you're looking to release impulses, feelings, sensitivity. Without the mask. The mask has an attitude in it. Take off the mask, and the attitude that came with it. Okay? Begin. I'm going to take the blouse off, too.

ACTRESS: Oh, you wouldn't. Would you?

Class laughs.

ACTRESS: I mean, it's not...I don't have....

MILTON: I'm kidding. Sing.

Actress sings.

MILTON: Don't swallow. You're swallowing the emotion. Did you feel that emotion? It isn't going to come knocking on your door every day. Let it happen.

Actress sings, crying.

MILTON: Sing, come on. You're doing beautifully.

Actress finishes song.

MILTON: The idea is to remain open, the body and the face relaxed. Stanislavski said that at the highest moment of emotion the actor should be the most relaxed. How can you act if you have a tense mask? A set attitude. This is what we pick up from granny and mom. Attitude. In this exercise you get conscious of it, and drop the mask. A simple, professional exercise. Nothing to do with Freud, Jung, Sam Spade, or anyone else. Do you want to smile now?

ACTRESS: Yeah.

MILTON: Then do. Okay? We're going to do the second part. This is the part where the blouse really comes off. Kidding, kidding. I swear.

Laughter and smile from the actress.

MILTON: There you go. See the smile is different now. More free. It's more genuine.

ACTRESS: God, this is hard.

MILTON: Let's go into the physical part of the exercise. There's still more to come about this secret you've got. Dance. *(Actress starts moving)* Disco, jazz in one place, feet on the ground, move the body. Sing out. Okay. Good. Stop for a second.

She stops.

MILTON: Now tell me about movement. Is there something about not being too sexy in dancing, and by all means don't put your skirt up over your head?

ACTRESS: Well, my mom taught me dancing.

Class laughter.

MILTON: I knew I'd hear that some day. And, of course, the first thing your mom said was *"Be wild and sexy, grind it out there,"* right? *"The priest is in the second row, turn him on."* That's what she said, right?

ACTRESS: She was my P.E. teacher, my English teacher, my Spanish teacher and my coach in junior high school. She taught me dancing. We used to do the cha-cha.

MILTON: Tonight is your chance to cut loose from that old cha-cha. Now, my feeling is there's a lot that you would like to do in dancing that you have never done. Are you prepared for that? No? We always have Spanish Fly in the office. Someone put a little bit of that in some water and she'll be ready.

Class laughs.

MILTON: In other words, you've got to be ready to turn on the juice when they call you, without Spanish Fly. Do you understand? Hello?

ACTRESS: I know what it's leading up to and....

MILTON: You're afraid to do it?

ACTRESS: Yeah.

MILTON: Just sing. Now jump. Jump! Let go.

Actress jumps, sings, and discos.

MILTON: Just move the body, don't worry about the singing. Keep going, tears come or whatever. If you die we'll tell them all about it, don't worry. Dance!

Suddenly the actress dances in a new way, free, sexy, alive, connected. A total change from the stilted dancing she had been doing up until this moment. The class responds and cheers.

MILTON: Now, you see what you can do. And you have a lot of courage. What you told us about your mother, nothing against mothers—but it's very hard for a mother—no matter how well-meaning, to train the daughter. They don't allow surgeons to operate on their own families, you know? So the mother trains her daughter to be a certain way: to avoid a certain sexuality, and to get closer to conventional, puritanical, beauty. *Comprende?*

ACTRESS: *Si.* But now what do I do?

MILTON: Just do your work. Do Maggie in *Cat on a Hot Tin Roof.* That'll help you bust out. Now, your secret. I told you I was going to find your secret.

ACTRESS: That my mom taught me how to dance?

MILTON: Yes, ma'am. That's the secret. The cha-cha.

Comedy is Serious Business

A woman loses it in the supermarket, acting just like Medea when killing her children: *"Where are the steel wool pads? I need SOS pads, WHERE ARE THE SOS PADS? I SHOULD TAKE YOU ALL TO COURT!"*

The lines themselves are not funny. But why might other shoppers who witnessed this meltdown repeat this story when they get home as something funny that happened to them? It's funny because the poor woman absolutely wants and needs the item, but has tipped over the scale of what is acceptable or understandable behavior. She has gone into a world beyond our comprehension, a desperate need like that of a drug addict. She has become a junkie, and the SOS pad has become the shot she needs to get high.

So what is comedy? It's real, yes. But it demands a highly evaluated point of view. One needs to look at it and understand what is humorous about what's taking place. Just as one sees what is particularly dramatic about a different event, you have to single out the humorous point of view. With the woman in the supermarket, the humor is that she so exceeds what we expect, she goes into another realm, and therefore it's humorous. It's the juxtaposition of the banal need for SOS pads and the ballistic expression of that need—that's what's funny. To some people she could be scary, but to many she's black comedy funny. So good comedy needs this point of view, and an understanding of that juxtaposition. In a drama like *Death of a Salesman,* we understand the essence of the piece, so that Willie Loman's suicide becomes a tragic moment. Obviously, the actor playing that role has to recognize this dramatic essence—and understand the play as a tragedy very specifically and clearly. Of course he doesn't necessarily play the tragedy, but he knows where the play is headed. In a comedy, *The Odd Couple,* Felix's overboard fastidiousness is absolutely true and real. The actor playing him should chase that in as detailed and serious a fashion as possible. Yet the actor knows that the outcome he wants is humorous. Ditto with the sloppiness of Oscar. It's the absolute reality of those characteristics, and then the *contrast* of these two, the collision of their opposite points of view that creates humor. So even when the sensibility of the writer is comedic, where the lines themselves are funny, it still requires the actors to discover that specific point of view and chase it relentlessly, and with a feverish reality. A clever line can only go so far when not backed up by the actor's evaluation and delineation of point of view. That's why Neil Simon almost always chooses really skilled actors, rather than just comics, to bring his plays to life.

Remember Charlie Chaplin doing that bit in *The Gold Rush,* where he is so hungry and has nothing to eat, so he boils a shoe and eats the shoe? He doesn't "wing it." He eats that shoe in a very meticulous fashion—the shoe strings become spaghetti, the sole becomes a piece of steak, and his hunger makes this shoe appear to him to be something quite delicious. All of that is made very real by the actor. The performance has the relish and specificity of a real meal. The humor comes from the juxtaposition of those two specific realities: A dirty old shoe, a starving Chaplin—and then the guy eating it with such relish and satisfaction.

More recently, in the television series *Everyone Loves Raymond,* all of those actors had a certain approach towards being real. And they're all fine actors. One of them, Doris Roberts, created a real woman from a part that could have been the clichéd, strident, Italian mother—she gave her a real and three-dimensional quality, a certain delicacy that compensated for the potential acerbic quality of the character. She found a quality of voice that was gentle, rather than harsh. She based her choices on the real love a mother feels for her sons, rather than on the cleverness of the lines. The relationship between her and her husband, played by the excellent actor Peter Boyle, was also based very much on a reality—a couple seemingly ill-suited to each other, but yet married for decades—and the humor came from that truthful, colorful relationship.

Or Jackie Gleason as Ralph Kramden in *The Honeymooners:* When he gets angry at Alice, he's really angry. It's not a "comedy" anger, it's a real anger, but he expresses it just a bit differently. Gleason understands that Kramden doesn't have the physical tendency really to hit her. He is, at the base of it, a sweetheart. The best he can do is to lift his fists to the gods: "Alice, one of these days.... Pow, to the kisser!" Furious, yes, but he swings at the air. That's the humor. So unlike Stanley Kowalski, who fights physically, and destroys things, Kramden, infuriated by Alice, takes that real anger and expresses it hilariously. But it's Gleason's job to ensure the anger is authentic, alive, evaluated, and specific.

When Cary Grant's character in *Bringing Up Baby* is upset, super careful about his dinosaur, he's extremely fastidious and very serious about hours and days and weeks of work he put into the project. He knows that she is going to do something terrible with this dinosaur—he senses that. Keeps telling her to be careful, even though he knows by now in his experience with her that she will continue to fuck things up. The understanding of that specificity is crucial. When he responds to her destroying it, he is seriously disturbed, but he knew it was coming. It's real. And really funny.

Everyone has a sense of humor—some have it more naturally than others, some have to develop it, but either way you need to encourage that sense, go with it, allow it to blossom. So when you approach comedy, utilize that sense of humor and truthfully approach the reality of the situation. Be fully aware of its comedic possibilities, and devote yourself to creating a real person, keeping in mind that opposites attract, and opposites are possibly funny. Don't just perform some odd and peculiar behavior that's ridiculous and that you think will be funny. Look for that reality, that truth. You may do some ridiculous things, but do them seriously. So the old expression, "Comedy is a serious business" is true.

Tough Love

Torch Song Trilogy

ACTOR: I've canceled this scene about seven times. I was told I have a year to live last May. I have cancer. It's like...I wanted to do the scene perfect. Every time I rehearsed, it wasn't perfect. This is it. I wanted to be good this last time. And I feel I was. I've come here on Saturdays, even during my chemotherapy, which is just brutal. Saturdays have been God's gift. I could look forward to Saturday class. I feel very good inside, despite all these tears.

MILTON: I really understand. But I just want you to know, you'll get a straight up critique.

ACTOR: That's fine. If I beat this, my God, I can do the scene again. I did a drag queen part in a movie for Cassavetes. During my research, I met many female impersonators from La Cage Aux Folles—the club over on La Cienega. My character, in this *Torch Song Trilogy,* is from Brooklyn. I worked on the accent, but I also tried to find something from within my own life to put me in the scene. Doing this means a lot to me today. This is hard.

MILTON: I understand. You got the female impersonator down wonderfully. You have the relationship. You're touching, you're emotional, you're funny. But you put too much self-pity in the character. What you need in the part is more street, more down to earth. It is a cover for Arnold's sensitivity and his hurt. The toughness, the street thing. The guy that wrote *Torch Song* works as the character in it because of his voice. The voice is a truck driver. Now I don't mean you should be a truck driver; I mean, it's street, tough and protected. The sensitivity is behind it.

ACTOR: He's very Brooklyn.

MILTON: There's a healthy, open, honest, no-bullshit thing about him. It surprises us because we've cast him in our mind as limp-wristed, pretentious. And it's the opposite. And it is a part of what he leads with in his whole life, as a protection. It's his cover. We think he's the kind of guy who's going to say, "Please, please support me, please accept me." Instead: "What's your problem, Mom? I'm a female impersonator." The toughness. Your thing in the scene with the boyfriend should be: "I'm goin' home, baby. Fuck you. I'm packin' up and I'm goin' home. I'm not getting caught up with you again." But he gets caught up. Like we all do. We get caught up in the relationship again. I'd love it if you take off your clothes in front of him with the attitude of, "What do you want?"

ACTOR (As Arnold): "What do you want from me?"

MILTON: Exactly. Streetwise to the point of almost black-comedy cruelty. He says to the guy, "So you almost killed yourself? So maybe you shoulda finished the job."

ACTOR: At La Cage, there's this famous guy who's the M.C., his name is Gypsy, and he is tough. And he goes, "Oh, hello, everybody. Fuck you all."

MILTON: Yeah. That's right.

ACTOR: He says to someone in the audience, "Oh, are you going to the bathroom? Don't forget, lid up, honey!" You know, all that kind of tough stuff.

MILTON: Exactly.

ACTOR: But I didn't work on that enough. I thought the M.C. was a great example from the school of "Honey, you think just because I'm in this dress, I'm a fairy? I'll beat the shit out of you."

MILTON: That's right, tough. Arnold asks, "Is the girl better in bed than me?" It's honest. He's asking the tough questions.

ACTOR: They're hard to answer.

MILTON: Yeah. You'd like to roast the fucker.

ACTOR: I want my lover to talk to me honestly.

MILTON: And you'd like him to suffer his ass off. Finally, the lover breaks down. He can't stand not to have you. When you say, "Get the hell out of here, I don't want you," he just can't stand not to have you, not to be with you. So he breaks down and confesses, and then he gets to you.

ACTOR: But I never let him forget for a minute what he is—a two-timer. "Don't bullshit me."

MILTON: Exactly. Make him suffer. But Arnold should still feel very emotional.

ACTOR: But I'm not gonna let him see it.

MILTON: Yeah. This is Arnold's foolishness. He opens himself up absolutely. It's like he says to his lover, "So, you wanna come back? Well, it's not gonna be that easy." That's where a little bit of your self-pity came in.

ACTOR: Yeah.

MILTON: I don't mind leaks, but there's fury in it too, along with the grief.

ACTOR: I want to make the lover pay for what I went through.

MILTON: Love fucks us over. We're all hooked by love, and it pisses us off. So don't be afraid to be angry in this part. Arnold should say about himself, "You weak son of a bitch."

ACTOR: So I play it drag, and then at times, I must come into being the person.

MILTON: The tough guy. And the drag queen. Both. You seem strong. You're not doing the chemotherapy right now?

ACTOR: Not for the last week.

MILTON: You've done a tremendous piece of work, very alive, energetic, courageous, humorous. Get it fully done. Do the scene again.

ACTOR: Sure. I can repeat the scene. Goddamned right.

MILTON: Yes. So go back to the M.C. at La Cage, get the tough street guy, the cover, and when you're ready, bring it back and kick ass. Any reason why not?

ACTOR: None. None whatsoever. Okay! I'll do it!

A Work In Progress

Two actors sit for their critique.

MILTON: Okay. Anything you want to say?

ACTOR: Well, we consider this a work in progress, you know. Just wanted to bring in what we've done so far....

MILTON: What does that mean? I've always wanted to know what this phrase means: "Work in Progress." Can you tell me? I really want to know. I hear it quite often.

ACTRESS: We didn't have much time to rehearse the scene, so....

MILTON: I still don't know what you mean. Either of you. What is a "work in progress"?

ACTOR: I've been slammed lately on the day job front, and then she had family in town, with, you know, obligations, so it was.... We didn't want to blow off the scene altogether.

MILTON: Who said anything about blowing off the scene?

ACTOR: Well it seems you're unhappy about "work in progress," but we had this time problem....

MILTON: There isn't a time problem. There isn't a family-in-town problem. There's a "work in progress" problem. It's the concept of "work in progress"—that's the problem. I see a piece of this attitude in almost every class. What is a work in progress? What if you have sex with somebody and you say, "This is a work in progress, baby!" Or you're cooking dinner, or washing your car, or doing your tax return. Do you tell the IRS that your return is a "work in progress"? Nope. You do these things fully.

ACTRESS: But how do you...?

MILTON (*Interrupting*): Committed work. The best work you're capable of. You have to explore all that you know before I can really contribute. Otherwise, it's a damn lie. You bring in a wreck that I try to repair, when you on your own can do better. You know what to do. Do it! You really want to know what I feel on a personal level, when scenes are brought in not fully worked on? I feel screwed. I've been had. Professionally, you wouldn't do this kind of work. Why do it here? Both of you know damned well that if some good money, some *gelt*, was at stake, you'd make it great. So make it better than great here, because this is bigger than *gelt*, and can lead to a lot of *gelt*. A single acting job pays you once. A good class and your commitment to it will result in the talent and ability to book many acting jobs. That's the importance of a class. Right?

Silence.

MILTON: When you work with Scorsese, after a take why don't you try saying, "Sorry about that, Marty, that was a work in progress." If you're committed, you'll create the time to do it right. And look, we have a shoot exercise where actors perform a scene without any rehearsal. When you do that, I don't expect any lower quality. So do a brilliant shoot or rehearse until you get it right. You're cornered. Time or no time, you've got to kick ass. But you both got "work in progress" in your head. It's not a good concept. Here's a good concept: "If I step foot on this stage, no matter how many rehearsals I had, I am going to throw down a fucking gauntlet and kill the scene. With fervor. And passion." That's much better, don't you think?

ACTOR *(reluctantly)*: Yeah. That sounds a lot better. Sorry we brought this in.

MILTON: It's not about sorry. It's about...look, do you always bust your ass to do good work? Yes. Whether it's a tiny garage somewhere or a hundred-million-dollar film, make the same effort. Don't do less. Bob Fosse once told me he was working as hard on a project he was doing in a garage as he did on a Broadway show.

Is there pressure on you? Yes. And I want it here because the pressure is there professionally. Comfort has nothing to do with art. Do I want every scene done fully? You're damned right. Even if that means you might have to give up some of your comfortable social life or beauty sleep. Listen, I think it's so true most of the time: Rehearsal is better than life. Wild, right? But think about it. Rehearsing a scene, getting in touch with your character, telling a story, figuring it out, communication with a good acting partner.... Yes. It's better than life. So dive in with some fucking passion and fervor and do your thing.

Why Isn't An Actor All He Can Be?

57 Varieties

1. I can't do it
2. I'm afraid
3. I don't believe I'm any good
4. It worked in rehearsal
5. My choices are bad
6. My choices are grotesque
7. My choices are embarrassing
8. My agent doesn't believe in me
9. My girlfriend doesn't believe in me
10. My boyfriend doesn't believe in me
11. I didn't wear the right dress
12. Fear
13. My partner's not any good
14. It's too hot out
15. It's too cold out
16. It worked in rehearsal
17. I'm psychologically blocked by my family
18. My family is psychologically blocked by me
19. I didn't pick this scene
20. I picked this scene but I didn't want to do it
21. I hate the part
22. I'm not a commercial type
23. I'm too commercial
24. It worked in rehearsal
25. I lost my concentration
26. I felt rushed
27. I didn't want to be in bad taste
28. I'm not sure I want to be an actor

29. My father doesn't want me to be an actor
30. My mother doesn't want me to be an actor
31. My husband doesn't want me to be an actor
32. My wife doesn't want me to be an actor
33. My sister doesn't want me to be an actor
34. My girlfriend doesn't want me to be an actor
35. My boyfriend doesn't want me to be an actor
36. I really don't want to be an actor
37. I have a terrible agent
38. My agent never calls
39. I can't even get an agent
40. It worked in rehearsal
41. My acting teacher doesn't believe in me
42. I don't believe in my acting teacher
43. I don't feel well
44. I'm not good enough
45. I'm just here to polish my work
46. I have to be perfect
47. I haven't booked a job in three months
48. Success scares me
49. Failure scares me
50. I'm overweight
51. I'm not pretty enough
52. I'm too pretty
53. No time to rehearse
54. My shrink said not to push
55. I don't want to
56. I don't know
57. It worked in rehearsal

The Director Is Not God

Adapted from a Colloquy on Directing
at Southern Methodist University:
An Actor Should Know What A Director Does

MILTON: How many of you are actors here? Okay, directors? Good. Excellent. I'm glad, because I think actors and directors don't talk enough, don't quite understand each other enough. So hopefully this talk will be beneficial for both sides. Anyway, diving in here, I looked up the word "direction."

> **direction**, n., pointing of thought or effect on a predetermined path or course.

Now here is a definition of a direction indicator, which I found to be one of the best definitions of what a director does:

> **direction indicator**, n., compass that assists an airplane pilot in flying a predetermined course by direct reading of two indicators, one which is set for the desired heading, while the other shows the actual heading, so that when the two indicators point alike the airplane is flying the desired course.

Isn't that terrific? That is what happens when you rehearse a play or do a film. At a certain stage of rehearsal, here (pointing) is where you are, and there (pointing elsewhere) is where you want to be. And if you can finally get those two together, you've done it. The director has got this target, this concept, this predetermined course, and he's got to get the actor and the whole design team aimed in that direction to deliver the product.

QUESTION: I find it really hard sometimes to talk to a director, and I was wondering what you thought of that?

MILTON: Well, as actors you may meet the wrath of God. Because while the director is not God, he may think he is. So you approach God and say, "In the second act you told me to have the funeral on my mind. What did you mean by that?" He says, "I can't talk to you now. I'm busy." Or he may just throw his cloak over his shoulder and not even speak to you. Just find the right moment to talk to him. Not when he's swamped. The right moment. Believe me, if you genuinely persist in a charming way you will get an answer.

And watch out—if you are trying to be right, to argue, to talk from the chip on your shoulder, it won't resolve. But if your intention is first and last to clear up the problem, then it will resolve. The quality of our work in theatre and film is based upon the quality of communication between the artists who are doing the work.

QUESTION: Doesn't effective communication depend on the readiness of people to be open to each other?

MILTON: Yes, but some people are not going to be open. You have to be ready for that. If you don't act on that information, your goose is cooked. And for you actors here, you are not some lowly person, you are one of the most important parts of the creative team. Act that way.

As a director, when you promise something, deliver. If you tell an actor you're going to get a certain costume, or you tell the cast you are going to improvise, do it, or else three weeks after you start, you'll be wondering why things are not working out. The answer is simple: You didn't deliver.

ACTING CLASS

If an actor thinks of an idea, don't take it for your own. Josh Logan taught me that one. Announce whose idea it was—acknowledge it. By the way, that is something few people do in the theatre: acknowledgments. Try it sometime. If a director gives you a suggestion, tell him, "That's a good idea." Watch him brighten up like a new penny. And as a director, if an actor does an interesting choice in the scene, come up to him and say, "Very good. That's good, no bullshit!" He brightens up.

QUESTION: How do you come up with a concept for a production?

MILTON: Well, when I read a piece of material, the first thing I try to do is understand the author. What did he have in mind? The author is a genius until proven otherwise. Proven otherwise. What did Shakespeare have in mind? Get the folios, the variorum. If the writer is alive, meet him. Talk to him, share his company. Find out what makes him tick.

I once read a script that started, "As Ann opens the refrigerator, a bicycle comes out." I say, wait a minute. This is a terrific play! And I wonder, is there someone on the bicycle? I start to think, maybe we could get a really small actor. This is a great first-act opening! I'm very excited and I read on eagerly, but I can't finish the first act. I call the writer. I say, "Look I'm reading your play. In the first scene there it says Ann opens the refrigerator and a bicycle comes out." He says, "No! No! That should read, *icicle*." I'm dead. I'm cut to the quick.

When reading the script, both directors and actors have to trust their instincts. You will have an immediate response: be aware of it, trust it. These first impressions

143

are what I try to be open to and spring off of. Some of them are crazy images: thoughts, flashes, places, memories, emotions. Whatever they are, I write them down immediately. They can be ephemeral and I don't want to lose them.

QUESTION: What about the communication with designers and such?

MILTON: The main thing you want to address with a designer is whether he or she has the right sensibility for your vision. When I directed *The Rose Tattoo,* I tried working with a designer who was referred to me by the great scenic designer, Boris Aronson, who had used him on *Cabaret.* We met a couple times at my place, and he kept bringing renderings that were totally off from what I had told him I wanted. Finally I decided to meet at his apartment to see more of his sensibilities. I walked in and I saw the whole problem: He had these glass stairs with lights underneath that turned on as you walked them, like a disco floor. The doorbell was a sculpture of a boxer. There were all these Paul Klee-like decorations— he had a totally different sensibility from what I needed. It was perfect for *Cabaret*, but not right for *Rose Tattoo.*

QUESTION: I am wondering why you don't design your own shows? Is the answer because you are not God?

MILTON: The fact of the matter is, I happen to be God, but I am talking about other directors. No, I don't design. I enjoy the communication with designers, I like the collaboration.

QUESTION: Is there a fixed process you use every time you set out to direct a play?

MILTON: A director is like a detective, you only get clues. I mean, it is very seldom that this goddamn concept comes marching up over the hill like some brigade of soldiers and says, "Here I am. This is what to do. It's a play about this!" Usually you search like hell until you get a flash.

A hunch is our creativity giving a hint. That's Frank Capra.

Here's an example: I was working on *Macbeth*. With any play I do that was done before, I read every review I can find of every production ever done—I find that to be a very informative exercise. So in reading the history of various productions, I realized that rarely had the witches really been brought off successfully. Most of the time, all that the witches ever did was make the audience laugh. So my thing was, how do you create a serious concept for witches? How to make them work?

I am not Leonardo da Vinci. It doesn't just suddenly come to me; I have to search. I have to look, and most of you in this room have to look. So don't be discouraged if you don't find it right away, or if you don't think it measures up to Leonardo's. Find your own. I knew that I didn't want the witches to be laughed at. They had to have power. They had to be reckoned with. I didn't know how to do this, so I looked at my own life for a key. Your life, your imagination is the whole ballgame. I remember I used to carry the golden staff for the Archbishop at the Greek Orthodox Church. When he entered from the altar the congregation became still, solemn, almost fearful. This is what I wanted for the witches. Power, ritual, mysticism. But how to connect the powerful Archbishop and the witches? Religion. Yes, it had to be something a little mystical. But how? So a few days later I saw a hooded nun just walking, and as I watched she seemed to eerily float. I'm on to it now. Nuns, the unknown, something scary. What the hell scares me? The dark is a little frightening to me, I have to admit it. I'm not totally happy about a pitch-black place.

The search goes on even more intensely. Sarah Siddons, the famous 18th century actress, when she did her legendary work in the role of Lady Macbeth, went into her attic with a candle, and tried to scare herself. So I break into the theatre at three o'clock in the morning. I turn off all the lights. Pitch black. I'm ill at ease. Now I don't smoke, but occasionally I take a cigarette. So I am walking across the creaky stage, smoking this cigarette. Suddenly, something comes up in front of my face. I literally jump about a foot and a half! It was the smoke. So what scares us? Shakespeare says in the play, "what is, is what is not." What appears as one thing is something else. The unknown. Religious ritual. Mysticism!

So now I got the whole thing. I run out of the building and drive recklessly to the designer's house. It's four o'clock in the morning, he's sleeping. I ring the doorbell and shout, "I've got it! I've got it!"

Practical: Nuns have hoods. We had to create a costume that had a hood on it. The material: jersey. Three colors: gray, black, dark olive. Nuns, hoods: perfect. The set: concrete, because we're doing it in Pittsburgh. I want to make a Pittsburgh Macbeth. So steel and concrete. When the witches wear jersey habits and stand against the cement, with the hoods sheltering their faces they seem to disappear. Suddenly Macbeth is talking and this thing, this apparition comes out of the wall. That's it. "What is, is what is not;" a wall becomes a witch. I wanted incantations. So that when they did the "Boil, boil," which is often a big laugh, the three of them, with serious, frightening, somewhat white faces, sat on this ledge, and incanted it like a Roman Mass. Backed by a Moog Synthesizer, it was scary. It was dynamite.

The procedure to arrive at that image, that concept, is a very logical, very simple one, that does not demand anything but to search for the key, and be open to the possibilities. All that's left is to communicate it to your fellow artists and then to the audience.

QUESTION: I'm one of the actors here in the crowd. I was wondering if you could talk about the difference between stage acting and film acting? I know you've worked in both fields....

MILTON: I don't see any difference. I don't buy into this whole film-acting, stage-acting dichotomy. Obviously when you're in a closeup on film, and the lens is 18 inches off your face, you can't move a lot, because you'll slide out of focus. Maybe a choice that works for a thousand-seat theatre won't work for a closeup, but that doesn't mean the acting is fundamentally different. The work is the same. The emotions are the same. The degree of emotion is the same. The story is the same. You're in love with a girl, you want to kill the king, you're going to rob that bank—whatever it is, these story points are the same. A professional, experienced actor knows how to modulate his level of expression, whether from being in a different sized theatre or being on film, but that's the same as with any performing art. Singers sing differently for a small room versus a big hall, but that doesn't mean you have "big hall" singers and "small room" singers. I don't buy it. And I don't really buy it for acting either. Acting is acting. A pro can act in any environment: closeup, long shot, one-camera, three-camera, small theatre, big theatre. And I think the whole "film acting" thing, when it's thought of as a completely different way of acting, that can be confusing, in the sense that it can scare the actor, make him possibly refute the basic truths of his work that he knows, and even limit him from making the bold choice.

A perfect example of this issue is the actress Eileen Heckart, whom I directed on Broadway in *Butterflies are Free.* I then directed the film version, and she played the same part. And she did what many might do—she wanted to lessen the choices, make her performance "smaller for film." *Do less for film,* or whatever that is. I looked at the first day's work on film, the rushes, and the performance wasn't there. It didn't pop at all. I went right up to her the next day and told her to play the part the same as she had on stage, not to change a damned thing. She ended up winning the Academy Award for that role. When I mention Academy Awards, that gets your attention, right?

Look, the great performances—the great film performances, I don't think you can say these are small performances, just simple naturalism. When Brando screams, "Stella!" in *Streetcar Named Desire,* that ain't just naturalism. Or Pacino in *Dog Day Afternoon.* Or Streep in *Sophie's Choice.* And it's not just the classics— look at last year. Daniel Day Lewis in *There Will Be Blood,* or the French actress, who was it, Marion Cotillard in *La Vie en Rose.* These are full-throated, hot-blooded, go-for-broke performances.

QUESTION: What first got you into the arts?

MILTON: Well, growing up, my father owned a movie house with a pool room downstairs. I saw all the movies, I was involved with booking the films for the theatres, and was always obsessed with having a full house, which is good trait for directing. I thought I might want to act, which didn't exactly thrill my father. I went to Carnegie Mellon, but I had trouble with the phoniness, the airs. I was a basketball player. When I walked around the campus, there were actors with long flowing scarves floating through the halls. And there I was with a crew cut. Just a basketball player, wondering, "What the hell is all this jazz?" I ran my father's pool room at night, with very elite clientele like Beansie, Green Cat, Tappers and Chipso—nice guys, but real street life. And by day I'm with the scarved set studying to be an artist, and not sure I deserved to be one.

The scarves were doing Moliere and Shakespeare in a highly stylized way. Then I realized: This high style is what *they* want to do. Not what *I* want to do. I had something else in mind for myself: A career of doing plays by Williams, Miller or any writer where knowing the street was important. At that moment, I knew I had my door into the art. And even though I had this sports background, the poolroom background, I learned to love the scarves. One of my friends at university was gay. A lot of the engineers and jock types at school figured I was gay too, because my friend was this really flying-three-feet-off-the-ground kind of guy. But I liked him and we would laugh and joke and I would imitate his flights and he'd imitate my macho ways. Sometimes I would borrow a scarf from the costume department and we'd go flying, arm in arm, into the cafeteria, which was packed with engineers, architects, jocks, and other macho types. I didn't give a damn. So that was all kind of the beginning of my trip, which then took me to New York, and everything that happened from there.

In closing, I'd like to read you something. This is what the artist has to nurture and protect:

> *To believe your own thought, to believe that what is true for you in your private heart is true for all men—that is genius. Speak your latent conviction, and it shall be the universal sense, for the inmost in due time becomes the utmost—and our first thought is rendered back to us by the trumpets of the Last Judgment. Familiar as the voice of the mind is to each, the highest merit we ascribe to Moses, Plato, and Milton, is, that they set at naught books and traditions, and spoke not what men but what they thought. A man should learn to detect and watch that gleam of light which flashes across his mind from within, more than the luster firmament of bards and sages. Yet he dismisses without notice his thought, because it is his. In every work of genius we recognize our own rejected thoughts: they come back to us with a certain alienated majesty. Great works of art have no more affecting lesson for us than this. They teach us to abide by our spontaneous impression with good humored inflexibility then most when the whole cry of voices is on the other side. Else, tomorrow a stranger will say with masterly good sense precisely what we have thought and felt all the time, and we shall be forced to take with shame our own opinion from another.*

That's Ralph Waldo Emerson from *Self Reliance.*

God doesn't have to go through this process. Directors, like most actors, not having yet attained this omnipotence, must toil and struggle and go through hell to reach heaven, where they will still only have visiting rights.

Arbitrary Choices

Uncle Vanya

MILTON: You just go and open the window.

ACTRESS: So what should I do?

MILTON: Anything, but don't just open the window, blindly following the author's instructions. There was no reason why. Is she sick, so she needs air? There was no surprise. How? Why? You just go like a mechanical puppet and open the window! Damnit!

ACTRESS: Why are you so pissed off?

MILTON: There's no surprise, no life, no arbitrary choice!

ACTRESS: So we can really question what the author tells us, the lines, the stage directions. In a sense put the lines on trial, as opposed to the lines dictating what we do?

MILTON: Of course the lines are on trial. Don't play the lines. Kazan said, "The play lies in the subtext." The lines are only one route to help you understand the possibilities. Don't just satisfy the text. Many people think the author is untouchable, and that the only thing you fulfill is what the dialogue describes. But I feel if you only do that, you're actually letting the author down. Anyone here have that Chekhov quote? Yeah? Go ahead.

STUDENT *(reading):* Anton Chekhov: "Never be afraid of an author. An actor is a free artist. You ought to create an image different from the author. When the two images—the author's and the actor's—fuse into one, then a true artistic work is created."

MILTON: And he's a pretty good writer. He has a sitcom deal over at CBS. Oh, yeah, oh yeah—it's in this week's *Variety*. So what is Chekhov asking for? Your participation. And Tennessee Williams said about Kowalski, "I did not write what Marlon Brando played. I wrote another character—more primitive, less human, less comic, less vulnerable." Brando brought something else to the part, to the text: a new conception.

ACTRESS: So, we should make our own choices.

MILTON: Yes, opposite choices. Arbitrary choices. This becomes a tool to use so you can open up the possibilities. A painter friend of mine said, "I paint a picture in order to find out what it looks like." Most actors are painting what they already know, as if it were paint-by-the-numbers.

ACTRESS: That's great.

MILTON: Pick choices that are difficult to deliver, choices that challenge you. Choices that make you find new avenues of expression, original ways to express your character.

ACTRESS: What about a choice like: I'm going to crawl on my hands and knees? I can't think of a less appropriate choice.

MILTON: For what?

ACTRESS: For my entrance, in terms of loosening up and exploring the parameters.

MILTON: Yeah, but why use arbitrary choices in a ridiculous way? You're diminishing the real creative use of the arbitrary by not giving it substance, reality or logic.

ACTRESS: Oh. I have to give it all that? Okay. Supposing I chose to dance in a sort of a folk dance, you know. Is that an arbitrary choice? Logical, all that?

MILTON: Maybe. Towards what end?

ACTRESS: Say, that she is happy to be free for a moment.

MILTON: From her husband?

ACTRESS: Yes.

MILTON: Good. It's arbitrary. But there's substance, reality and logic. It's connected to the story. It's connected because this is a specific, but kind of wild reaction to her husband upstairs.

ACTRESS: It's connected with the circumstances.

MILTON: Right. Your imagination can run free, but it needs to be connected to the story, what's happening in the scene. You have to have that basis, but once you do, don't say, "Oh, no. That's ridiculous. She'd never do that." Don't doubt. Do it.

ACTRESS: I think I understand. But at what point do I say, "I'm not going to do the scene the way it's usually done"?

MILTON: Right away.

ACTRESS: First rehearsal.

MILTON: Yes. Right away. As a director, I want everybody to know immediately we're going in another direction, and demonstrate this new direction with a specific behavior, a specific action, right off. You need a strong choice. Go on the stage. (*Actress moves to the stage.*) Little experiment. Now, just walk around as you did, but put yourself in a minefield.

ACTRESS: Can I have a mine detector?

MILTON: No. (*In Russian accent:*) You have to walk carefully, or young Russian girl blown up in dining room.

Actress walks around carefully.

MILTON: I like it. The room becomes sacred. Your behavior sacred. Expressive. Fearful. A lot better than just walking over to open a window because the stage direction says that's what you do. So, do you have at least one new possibility for the opening?

ACTRESS: Yes. The arbitrary choice of a minefield.

MILTON: Actors should act like human beings. Human beings are very unpredictable creatures. Many actors are worried about whether they seem "natural" enough, but too much of this concern leads to a lack of imagination. A lack of risk taking. Okay, I'll say it: I'm bored by it. I'm bored by a lot of acting I see. Too "natural." Too muted. No vibrancy. And yet you walk down the street and go to 7-Eleven and see this crazy shit going on. And in your own lives, you guys go to parties and you're out there, you're wild, you're doing these crazy things. But then in your acting, it stays safe, natural. So, oddly enough, the conventional choices make you act like actors, not people.

People are arbitrary. They'll do the wildest things, *in the name of something they want.* That's the trick. There's something they want—how they go about it may not seem logical, but in some way it is true to what they want.

ACTRESS: I think I get scared because out there, the casting people are always like, "Less. Do less. Don't act so much. Just simple reality."

MILTON: Simple reality. Yeah. Listen, they're saying what they *think* will help the actor. And if you're reading for a courtroom scene and your line is, "Objection!"— well, I don't think you should walk across the courtroom as if it's a minefield. You have to be smart about material and what's required. But at the same time, tell Pacino in *And Justice For All* to "do less, don't act so much...." He'll kill you. There are courtrooms and there are courtrooms. The arbitrary choice will help you in certain courtrooms created by certain writers.

ACTRESS: Differentiate, you mean.

MILTON: You got it. Let's take the end of the scene: Sonja goes upstairs to ask her father if they can play the piano and sing, and Yelena waits. Who says she just waits? Because the author wrote down, "She waits"? What does she *do* while waiting? The author says the piano isn't played. Isn't it better for her to start to play? Isn't it better for her to sing? You can both sing together before Sonja goes upstairs. In a suppressed house, you sing quietly. Very touching, very sweet. And as Yelena starts playing fully, Sonja comes back, and her line is: "Father says no."

ACTRESS: We actually did that once in rehearsal.

MILTON: But you know that Emerson quote—unless you follow the little idea that comes to you, you'll have to applaud somebody else doing it. So risk. Discovery is part of the journey. Jack Lemmon said, "If I know how to play it when I get through reading the script, there is no sense in my doing it."

Images

Killing the Lamb

Shock yourself.
—Elia Kazan

MILTON: Do you understand this character that Lillian Hellman has written in *The Little Foxes?*

ACTRESS: I thought I did. My idea was that Regina fights to get what she wants.

MILTON: Good. But this is a *tour-de-force* part. This is not a subtle chambermaid. This is not a little disgusted woman. This is a deep, deep, reptile. You have to nail that image for yourself when you go for a part like this.

ACTRESS: But she has to have another side to her.

MILTON: Oh, to hell with the other side. What other side? You didn't give us the reptile side.

ACTRESS: I'm trying to explain.

MILTON: I understand. And I'm not letting you. I'm trying to play the part. I'm being Regina. You won't get a single word in. "This is my house. When do I get what I want?" Maniacal. Psychotic. She's certifiable. This is our Lady Macbeth. This is our Medea. This is a woman who stands and watches her husband's death. She kills him. How does she kill him?

ACTRESS: By telling him that she didn't love him when they got married, and she does not love him now.

MILTON: That's right. She fooled him and made him feel that there was love. "No! I was pretending. I hated you then." It kills him. She brings about a heart attack. Watches him crawl up the stairs, trying to get his medicine. She stands there, not moving, in effect saying, "Die. I won't help. Die." That's the part. It's not small. It's bestial. It's a classic role.

ACTRESS: I wanted to have compassion for her.

MILTON: Compassion? Do you think she's just some pleasant little Southern Belle? Maybe she can act that pleasant Southern Belle as a cover, but that's not what she is in her gut.

ACTRESS: I think she's had to fight.

MILTON: You're goddamn right she has to fight. But she is neurotic. At the very least. She cannot stand it when anyone says she can't have what she wants. She cannot stand it. She goes sicko. Nutso. This is a wild, neurotic, diva of a part. This is not some put-a-dainty-blouse-on, pearl-necklace, hair-up kind of part.

ACTRESS: Is there a vulnerability at all?

MILTON: Yes. But not at this moment. He is dying and says, "Regina, help me." She doesn't move. How evil can you be? Hell, this is *The Little Foxes,* where they bite and eat each other for the spoils. It's desperate, it's bloody, it's the author's view of capitalism—people trying to devour each other for the money. So Regina is living that neurosis: "I'm willing to be as evil as I need to be to get what I want. I deserve it." This is America where money and power are everything. Now, you're a talented actress, but you don't want to play these strong, primitive characters. You avoid them, you pretty them up.

ACTRESS: I try to be reasonable. I want to see both sides of a person.

MILTON: But your thing about seeing both sides—it leads you to miss the main point here with *this woman*. Very few people in this room will ever murder someone, thank God. Regina murders this man. She breaks his heart, splits his valves apart and then refuses to get his medicine. So trying to find her vulnerability is not what's going to lead you—particularly you—to her center, her truth. You have to nail the killer before you worry about her "other side." Teaching acting depends on whom you're talking to. I'm talking to you, and this is very specific to your tendency—this humanitarian, see-both-sides, compassionate way of yours.

ACTRESS: So what do I do now in terms of looking at....

MILTON: Don't know so goddamned much. Don't try to figure acting out mentally, don't try to be so humanitarian and diplomatic—finding both sides. Not always. I remember rehearsing the scene in *Othello* where he kills Desdemona. The actor and I didn't know what to do after he kills her. There's a knocking at the door, and we thought, "Now what?" So I turned out all the lights in the theatre. People and actors are often freer in the dark. I whispered intensely to the actor, "What are you going to do? What? They're knocking on the door. You've killed her. Hurry up!" The actor didn't know what to do. He was confused. Suddenly he chose desperately to hide the body. But where the hell is he going to put her? He panics. He doesn't know. Madness!

And they're knocking. No place to put her. So he takes her, and he sits down, and he's cradling her in his arms and he starts to rock her like a little girl. Crying because he still loves her. We found this moment through not knowing what to do.

Sometimes I speak of the fabric of a part. The essence of a part. Not the character biography. Too much work is being done by talented actors on character biography. A very brilliant and successful actress in my class once played the empress in *Anastasia.* She found photos of the actual Romanov family, and created a fantastically detailed copy of that for her makeup and hair and costume. She looked like the real empress for sure. One problem. It wasn't her empress. She didn't quite have the fabric of the part, the essence—because she had sort of disappeared into certain biographical and visual information. Johnny Depp seems to take the fabric of his parts as written, but adds his own personal twist, his own ingredient that gives it all a kind of magic. George C. Scott—he won the Academy Award for *Patton,* but the fact is he created his own character that was not a copy of the actual Patton at all—but he understood the *essence* of Patton, that fabric, that certain obstinacy.

So who is Stanley Kowalski, really? Get some booze in him and he's violent, but he's also a pussycat with his wife. Or Sean Penn's character in *Mystic River,* violent on the one hand, but sending money to the family of someone he killed—Penn knows how to play that duality beautifully. Or Blanche Dubois—the juxtaposition of the debutante and the whore. The actress playing that part needs to put those two pieces of fabric together. Here, with Regina— that reptile, that murderess, the woman who can kill her husband and watch him die in front of her. You, especially—you have got to nail that first, for sure.

Acting is not mental work. Acting is not just "understanding." Acting is often letting go of understanding, of too much thinking, so that you can experience. Acting is emotional, and sometimes bloody. So here you need to find some images and feelings that can knock your socks off about your husband. Your deep resentment. Hatred.

You need images to act. When I was a kid, we used to have lambs that my father would get and kill, and we would eat them on festive occasions. Sweet lambs that we fed and cared for, and then—whack! The throat. You see? Images. What do these lambs have to do with *The Little Foxes*? In the scene, your husband is the lamb. Regina is looking right down the blade at his death. The husband is still kicking, still alive. She doesn't flinch. She's not affected. She kills him. Images.

Lena

Singing Exercise

MILTON: Did you watch the Lena Horne video I told you about?

ACTRESS: I did. I hated it.

MILTON: What didn't you like?

ACTRESS: I felt it was too affected.

Milton turns to the other students in the room.

MILTON: Nobody moves, I got the room covered. *(Back to actress:)* Affected, huh?

ACTRESS: Yeah.

MILTON: Hang on, folks, this could be major. Tell us your idea of affected.

ACTRESS: Put-on. Not done from the heart.

MILTON: Phony?

ACTRESS: Yes.

MILTON: Lena Horne?

ACTRESS: In this, she was.

MILTON: Anything else? You're already on your way to Siberia. I guess my connection with the Mafia didn't work. They were supposed to threaten your nieces and nephews, straighten you out.

Beat.

I don't get big laughs here because people think I really am connected to the Mafia. Okay, what else didn't you like about Lena?

ACTRESS: I felt at times that she was very bitter towards white people.

MILTON: So? What's wrong with that? I understand that point of view.

ACTRESS: Well, I didn't like it.

MILTON: Let me tell you why I think you really don't like her: Because she's ballsy. Out there. Willing to be counted. These are all aspects you have within you, but that you're fighting. Lena doesn't fight against herself. She communicates, and doesn't apologize for it. Your criticism keeps you away from these qualities that she has. You criticize her so you don't have to do the things she does. What you criticize you can't get.

Actress starts crying.

MILTON *(Ironically):* I guess I should cry, too, because apparently I've totally missed the mark here, haven't I?

Actress laughs through the crying.

MILTON: Don't you see? Lena is putting it all out there. Everything. She's sexual, she's openly emotional. She lets it all hang out. She can be anything she wants. She's a goddess. She's bitter about whites. So what? She's not censoring.

ACTRESS: No, not any of it.

MILTON: She's out there cracking the whip. You can't not like her. You, especially, have to like her. She is landmark audacious. You've got to be inspired by her. You've got to say, "Let my hatred of blacks out, my hatred of whites out, my love of blacks out, my love of whites out, *everything* out." Let everything out. What are you saving it for?

ACTRESS: I'm not loose at all. I protect myself. I am so uncomfortable in front of an audience.

MILTON: Okay. Tell us these awful things the audience can do to you, your nightmare.

ACTRESS: Go to sleep.

MILTON: They could go to sleep. Good. What else?

ACTRESS: They could yawn. Or laugh. You know, like laughing uncontrollably.

MILTON: I see. What else?

ACTRESS: They could leave.

MILTON: The ultimate. Leave while you're singing. I got you. Is there anybody when you look out there, that you feel doesn't want you to be a star?

ACTRESS: You mean right here in the class?

MILTON: No, over in Canoga Park. Yes—here in the class. Right here.

ACTRESS: I know somebody.

MILTON: Who?

ACTRESS: You mean, point them out?

MILTON: That's what Lena would do.

ACTRESS: Oh god....

MILTON: Do it. Go ahead, do it.

ACTRESS *(Pointing to a student):* I think she thinks I take too much time in class. She's like, "This is an acting class—why are we spending time on singing?"

MILTON: And your response?

ACTRESS: That I'm a singer *and* an actress. And this is my class, too. Music is a big part of me, and so this is part of my trip.

MILTON: Good. Pretty clear. No one collapsed or anything from you saying that. The theatre is still standing. Anything else you want to say to her?

ACTRESS: I think she envies me—the way I sing, the way I look. Part of why I'm studying acting is to bring myself out so I'm a better singer. I'm sorry if that disturbs anybody.

MILTON: Good. *(Indicating another student)* What about him?

ACTRESS: I think he doesn't care. I feel as I'm singing that he's totally disinterested. Bored.

MILTON: Okay. Pretty clear.

ACTRESS: God, everybody's going to hate me after this!

MILTON: You want to know something funny? The only way to really be loved is to say how you feel. When you're honest, people trust you. Like Clark Gable in *Gone With the Wind:* "Frankly my dear, I don't give a damn." And we love him for saying it. This is also about not being afraid to be disliked. Do you think Lena's worried all the time about who likes her?

ACTRESS: She couldn't give a shit.

MILTON: Anybody else?

ACTRESS: No, no. That's enough.

MILTON: Very good. See? And you haven't died yet. Good. In every audience, by the way, there is every person in the performer's life. Literally or in your mind, your father's here, your mother's here, your boyfriend, your girlfriend, everybody's here. So the idea is to train yourself not to be afraid of an audience. Say to them what you feel, be audacious, don't hold back. Connect with them and affect them. Be open. Say to them what they can't say to themselves. Your feelings and your singing must hit them where they live.

ACTRESS: Right.

MILTON: What would you like to say to this august body? About your singing, about you, about your life.

ACTRESS *(Getting emotional)*: I care too much. I care too much that you like me. And I can't care anymore because it's killing me.

MILTON: Sing now. While you're full of emotion. Come on, sing that song.

Actress sings. She's emotional, strong, more alive in her performance than she's ever been.

MILTON: Come on, that's it, keep going....

Song ends, to huge applause.

MILTON: Alright. Understand? Lena did that every night of the week.

Attitude

Attitude Opens the Door

Why does an acting teacher talk about attitude, dedicate a whole section of his book to it?

> **attitude**, n., The self-evaluation, emotional response, and state of mind that determines a person's energy output, degree of involvement, confidence, and creativity towards an action or undertaking.

But I really like this one:

> **attitude**, n., the orientation of an aircraft relative to its direction of travel

So if your attitude is off, you're not going to get to your destination. It's that simple. I don't like to teach acting in a vacuum. I like people to achieve what they're after. And if there's anything I've observed over the decades of teaching and directing, is that talent is not the only game in town. A mastery of the craft of acting is certainly Goal #1, but I've found that attitude is a major factor in the equation. Why?

As I said early in the book, an actor's attitude monitors his talent. Attitude lets the talent come through, using again the metaphor of how the aperture of a camera monitors the amount of light. The more healthy the attitude, the larger the aperture, the more light comes through. A good, confident attitude will support the smallest talent or technique. And here's an unpleasant reality (or pleasant, depending on your point of view): Just 10% technique, 10% talent, and 80% positive attitude can lead to a generous career. This is backed up by Kazan, who said that 80% of this business is the ability to get along with people.

"I am who I am and that's it. This is the way I have been and so be it. I tend to complain, gossip and argue. That's me. It's too late." This is all nonsense. Can a faulty attitude be improved? Absolutely. Change is possible. Start now. The first thing is to be aware. Awareness is what singles out human beings as special, capable of change. Something is wrong and it's not your talent or the role. It's your negativity that's stopping you—your attitude, the moody way you are doing things, the no joy, the being downbeat, not energized. You're roasting yourself. If you know that, you're already 25% of the way there.

Be aware of the way you do simple activities: The attitude you use to rehearse, to do your day job, the way you are with loved ones, how you prepare for your auditions, what energy you bring to class.... Each of these and all else should be done with an upbeat, interested, positive attitude. And if you see this is not the case, use your effort and will to change it. Neither your career nor your talent will survive unless you get your attitude straight with these everyday activities. The day-to-day attitude fans out and then affects every situation you're involved in, and this habit becomes your way of life. Are you, with these activities, giving it all? Are you bringing a winning attitude to your rehearsals and auditions? If not, you must make it your business to change and bring that added energy to your life and work. Don't be stubborn about this. Change is possible. Make the effort. It's the core of your life.

You'll notice in the essays and critiques to come a lot about the negative side of this—how the attitude can go off the rails and start to send the actor to a winter in Buffalo instead of Bermuda. I'm not trying to be negative. But I'm hoping that in the illustration of the negative attitude, you may see some aspect of yourself or someone you know, that you might say, "Ah...I have a bit of that, he's right, that bastard...."

The positive attitude? Well, when it's in front of you it's as clear as its opposite. Open. Willing—willing to listen, willing to learn, willing to be directed. A sense of humor, about oneself, about this nutso business, because otherwise you won't survive it. Charm. A smile. No hostile chip on the shoulder. A thirst for rehearsal, a diligence and discipline there. Gets along great with people, doesn't assert a rightness, just finds out how to communicate with each individual in an effective way. Good habits on the health front—not too much sugar, eating right, exercise, sleep, so the mind and the body are sharp.

So your incontrovertible, melodic attitude beat should be arranged to these notes: *ganas,* Spanish for *desire.* And bring some passion. And belief. Make the effort to win and persist, be your own friend, and head passionately towards your goals. After all, you are the boss. And believe in yourself. You can do it. Come on, you deserve success, right? Go for it. Don't let anything, I mean anything, block you. So let's go. No negativity, no excuses, no flinch, no lack of work ethic. A good attitude is a choice, and its sweet melody rings within you, as you simply move ever forward. Like the flivver in *Grapes of Wrath,* it gets the shit beaten out of it and it just keeps going, and so like Steinbeck's characters, you move, undaunted, step by step towards your goals.

Stanislavski On Ethics

Excerpted from <u>*Building a Character*</u>

The actor needs order, discipline, a code of ethics not only for the general circumstances of his work, but also and especially for his artistic and creative purposes.

If we keep our theater free from all types of evil we, by the same token, bring about conditions favorable to our own work in it. Remember this practical piece of advice. Never come into the theater with mud on your feet. Leave your dust and dirt outside. Check your little worries, squabbles, petty difficulties with your outside clothing— all the things that ruin your life and draw your attention away from your art.

People are so stupid and spineless that they still prefer to introduce petty, humdrum bickerings, spites and intrigues into the place supposedly reserved for creative art.

Does it not seem irrational to you to tear down with one hand what you are trying to build up with the other? Yet many actors do that very thing. On the stage they make every effort to convey beautiful and artistic impressions and then, as soon as they step down from the boards, almost as though they had been intent on spoofing their spectators who a moment ago were admiring them, they do their best to disillusion them.

The actor is still bound in his everyday life to be the standard bearer of what is fine. Otherwise he will only destroy what he is trying to build. Remember this from the very beginning of your term of service to art and prepare yourself for this mission. Develop in yourselves the necessary self-control, the ethics and discipline of a public servant destined to carry out into the world a message that is fine, elevating and noble.

Constantin Stanislavski

Personal Confidence

MILTON: So. What do you get out of doing this personal monologue?

ACTRESS: I don't know yet. I was so nervous I felt like I was going to vomit....

MILTON: Unimportant. Cut that line from the movie. Do you think you do a good job as an actress in this? Is this acting?

ACTRESS: No.

MILTON: I see. Why? What makes it not acting?

ACTRESS: Because it's pretty much true.

MILTON: So in other words, if you do something that is true, then it's not acting. So therefore we have to kill *A Chorus Line,* which was made by real people talking about their lives. So we kill that.

ACTRESS: No. Okay. I guess it's acting.

MILTON: You've got another twenty-eight seconds to say whatever else you want to say. Twenty-five.... Twenty. Try to shorten your acting training. Fifteen....

ACTRESS: I'm in a panic now, Milton.

MILTON: Eight.

ACTRESS: It was a big risk. More than I'm used to taking.

MILTON: I'll give you four more seconds as a reward for that one. How's the acting in this? Three, two....

ACTRESS: Okay.

MILTON: One. Flunk. You've added six months on to your training. Maybe a year. In the critique, we're here to find out what you were trying to do and how you feel about your work. Do you have a P.S.?

ACTRESS: Okay. In general, how I feel? *(Barely audible)* Good. I did good.

MILTON: Wow. Thanks for that. You're so far off, it makes me wonder if there is a chance to convince you. Because in the end, an artist has to have self-confidence.

ACTRESS: Well, that's what I want to get.

MILTON: Very good. So, let's have some comments. Yes?

STUDENT 1: It was great. You were absolutely brilliant. You touched me, you plumbed yourself, and in doing this you gave us an incredible acting lesson. And if your work here isn't acting, I don't know what the hell acting is. And you've got to know that.

MILTON: So what do you think about that, in comparison to "good?"

ACTRESS: I feel surprised. I do. I don't know what "plumbed" means.

STUDENT 1: You reached down into yourself. To plumb your depth is to reach into yourself.

MILTON: She doesn't get it.

ACTRESS: No, I do think I did go deeper.

MILTON: Oh. Well, how good a job did you do with this plumb, from your point of view?

ACTRESS: Eighty percent.

MILTON: I think you're being very careful now to make sure you don't entice our wrath with that 80%. I don't think you felt 80% at all. Good is not 80%. Good is maybe 60%, or 70%.

ACTRESS: Okay. Very good then.

MILTON: But that's not the idea. You can't hire us to follow you through life and encourage you. *(Indicating another student:)* You're dying to tell her something?

STUDENT 2: I just wanted to say that you're a real artist. I mean there's a hundred percent of you exposed. You have to know that, or else you're back to square one.

MILTON: How do you answer that?

ACTRESS: Thank you.

MILTON: But this is the fifth or sixth time this has happened, where we've had to tell you how good you are. How many times can we do that?

ACTRESS: I don't want to say I was so great because if it was bad, then I'd be full of shit.

MILTON: But honey, you're full of shit right now! You're not going to grow if you keep minimizing what you do. You stood there on the stage boldly and cleared up what you wanted to say to your father, your mother and your brother. You dug into yourself. You acted the hell out of it. You stood there open, and as bold as Antigone. That's the deal. That's what he means when he tells you that you're an artist. And you say meekly, "I was good." We don't need this kind of false modesty. We need you to know that you're a most confident, talented artist.

ACTRESS: That's right.

MILTON: I liken all this to a passport. The actor needs to validate his own passport. Just as you get a passport to travel in a country freely, so an actor issues himself a passport to travel the territory of the character. No one can do this for you—not me, not the critic, not the paycheck, not publicity, not the producer. None of them. The actor has to stamp it himself. I'd like to have a hundred bucks for every trip I've made to a dressing room or to a trailer to assure the actors how good they are. So don't tear it up. Keep validating it. It's your artistic passport, so stamp it and keep it close to your heart.

ACTRESS: Actually, I think I need to renew my passport.

MILTON: Wow. Humor! Good. Now, there is a myth in the world that if you don't have this insecurity, this so-called modesty, this plain neurosis, you can't be a great artist. I think that's the biggest crock that ever came along the pike.

ACTRESS: I don't want to be an asshole, I really don't.

MILTON: Some part of you wants to be an asshole. It's certainly running for office. You do a fabulous monologue here. One of the best I've ever seen. You moved these people. You delighted them. But you don't see it. You're more interested in your doubts and your fears and your questions. What this class is ultimately about is confidence. You have a gift. But you have to know the gift. Now listen carefully. See if you get this: You are one of the best actresses around.

She puts her head in her hands.

You're ashamed of that. This is the million-dollar prize. You won the sweepstakes. What?

ACTRESS: It makes me feel good. Truly.

MILTON: I see. This is good, huh? And you're crying. Can you imagine what she would do if you told her that somebody had stolen the tires off her car? You should be dancing! You should be celebrating. If they have good caviar in Los Angeles, which is questionable, and really good champagne, you should be treating yourself tonight. Tell us for keeps. Do you understand now?

ACTRESS: I do.

MILTON: Oh, yeah?

ACTRESS: I do, I do. Really. No really. I do. For keeps, this time.

MILTON: Oh, yeah?

I Wanna Do It Myself

MILTON: What are you so pissed off about?

ACTOR: I'm not pissed off.

MILTON: Really? You're not? So I'm wrong about that. You're not pissed off?

ACTOR *(Getting really pissed off)*: It's just...GOD. I just want to get it! It seems like I only get it when you help.

MILTON: Isn't the point to get it? To get the lesson? That's victory. Right? Who cares how you get it?

ACTOR: Right, yeah, I guess.

MILTON: Oh, now you're sulking. Pulling a little emotional tyranny on me?

ACTOR: What's that?

MILTON: Emotional tyranny? That's you, putting on a display of negative feelings to make me feel bad about what I'm doing. Students sometimes sulk to make the teacher feel bad about teaching. I've never experienced it personally. Oh, no. Let's just say I've read about it in books.

Class laughter.

ACTOR: Why are you picking on me?

MILTON: I'm not picking on you. Listen, I want my students to be able to direct themselves, because a lot of times you won't have a good director, or you may simply not get any direction at all—some people hide behind those video monitors or whatever and won't speak to you. But that doesn't mean you get all gloomy if help is actually at hand. We do it together. The whole industry is a group activity. Directors, producers, actors, writers, technical people...I listen to everyone. If the janitor tells me an idea, I listen. I don't give a shit. Why should you?

ACTOR: Maybe I'm pissed because you seem to get it so easily.

MILTON: That's experience. Don't resent experience. You've got to allow the teacher, the director, whomever, to participate. You're not alone in this attitude, by the way.

ACTOR: What attitude?

MILTON: What would you call it?

ACTOR: Let's see. Uh...I, uh...I guess...I wanna do it myself.

MILTON: Bullseye. It happens a lot. Too damned much. (*To the class:*) Your careers are going to be about you taking direction. From teachers, from directors. If you resent that process, you're going to have one hell of time of it. So, frankly, you all need to knock off the shit. I'm the one who's really pissed about this. This attitude is a damned disease. You understand disease?

CLASS: Yes.

MILTON (*pointing to another student*): What about you? No, you. Yes—that's right. You and I just did this dance, right? Last week? The Schisgal thing, *Luv?*

ACTRESS: Yes. When I left here after our work on *Luv*, I didn't take with me the joy of having just accomplished something. I felt I had just done a shit scene. I was glad you redirected it, but I didn't feel great. I only thought, "Why didn't I think of that myself?"

MILTON: You all hear that? There it is.

CLASS: Yes!

MILTON: It wasn't a "shit scene." The correction made you feel that way. When I redirected the scene, you felt like I just saved Spain. Spain was sinking and I saved it. This was not the case. It was not a badly acted scene even before I worked with you. We only made small adjustments. Really.

ACTRESS: Well, it's all relative....

MILTON: Relative, schmelative! I'm telling you it was not a bad scene. Yes, you improved when we worked on it. Yes, you were more vulnerable, more alive. But still, it was good before.

ACTRESS *(Sulking):* Okay...I mean...Okay.

MILTON: Oh, god. Are you going to start sulking, too?

ACTRESS: No.

MILTON: That's what you're doing right now. That's what you all do when you pull this "I Wanna Do It Myself" shit. Apparently tonight the disease is spreading.

Class laughs.

MILTON: Part of the thing we're dealing with here is that when you correct an actor and show them how their work could be better, you light up all the times in the past when they have been corrected and haven't liked it. Look, I want you to be your own artist. But theatre and film are communal arts. The heart and soul of the deal should be: "What information can I take from my teacher to better my work? Period." The same with directors. We work together. In a communal art we can't just do it ourselves.

This talk could fade from memory fast, and four weeks from now you'll retreat back to "I wanna do it myself." At that moment, stop yourself. Smile. A good little trick: Repeat the direction back to them. They ask you to go over to the desk or whatever, and you reply, "So you're saying you want me to go over to this desk, and...? No problem!" Because part of the disease is that you shut off from really listening. So stop. Smile. Repeat the direction. Acknowledge them. You can even say, "Great!" This trick allows you to settle down, and maybe you'll even thank the director for the help, maybe you'll find you're even a bit pleased. Look, I'm Greek. I just want to know you liked the grape leaves.

Laughter.

Let's take a break.

The Arrogance Of A Loser

In order to be all you can be....

MILTON: Could you just lower your chin a little bit?

ACTOR: Huh?

MILTON: Your chin. It's a little high. Your head is cocked back. You realize that?

ACTOR: No.

MILTON: You're looking at me as if you want to punch me in the face. You want to punch me in the face?

ACTOR: No.

MILTON: You're doing a good job of looking like you do.

The actor flashes a smile.

MILTON: Hey! A smile! Wow. That's better, much better. Let me ask you: the hostility, the chin, the head cocked back, the eyes narrowed, looking as if you're going to start a fight. What does it do for you? Other than keep people off your case. Or maybe that's the point. You don't like people on your case, right?

ACTOR: Not really. Never have.

MILTON: Yeah. Well, in acting, you need to let people get on your case. That's part of vulnerability. Everyone remembers Brando and the danger he brought to a lot of his work, the violence. But they forget the charm of the guy, how funny he was. How moved he could be by others getting on his case! In *On The Waterfront,* how he had a tear in his eye when Eva Marie Saint touched him in the bar scene. You ever get moved by the world around you? Like, by a rock or something, some beautiful rock?

ACTOR: Now you're making fun of me?

MILTON: See, this is part of it. The touchiness. Say the wrong thing, or even say the right thing, but in a slightly wrong way, and your kind of guy lights up. You can't be like this, my friend. You're a good-looking guy, you're talented, but this attitude—it creates a false arrogance— I call it, now don't kill me, please, the arrogance of a loser.

ACTOR: This is such bullshit.

MILTON: It's bullshit?

ACTOR: I don't get it. I don't get the arrogant part. I don't get the loser part. You think it's arrogant to know what you can do, to know you're probably better than most others? In my book, that's confidence. Isn't that what you've been talking to us about?

MILTON *(taking a beat)*: Sorry, I'm still recovering from the "bullshit" comment. But you got that right, yes—I want actors to feel confident. Maybe even for them to have a certain arrogance, which at its root means to "claim the space for one's own." But I'm sorry, my bullshit friend, this is not what you're about.

ACTOR: So tell me again, what is it that I've got?

MILTON: Sure. The arrogance of a loser.

ACTOR: Well that's your opinion.

MILTON: Well I thought that's what you've come here to this class to get. My opinion. Nobody asked you to come. You're requesting my services. So maybe, if you were able to, you should listen to me. It's simple. You ready? With you, the arrogance is that you take a sort of cocky attitude about your talent and pump it up and behave as if you're the be-all and end-all of acting when you're not. Not yet. And you know you're not. You're faking yourself out. I personally think you could be this great actor you think you are, if you could deal more honestly with where you are now, and build from there. You're not as good as you should be. You think this moody, broody, unaffected acting is the way in to the party, and it just isn't. Maybe you heard me, or maybe you didn't, when I spoke about Brando and his vulnerability. To be vulnerable, you have to let the chip down, get around the hostility. The loser part is that you're not being smart enough at this very moment to know you need to change. You're hostile, you're difficult to talk to. You look as if you want to start a fight. Arrogance. Loser. Is that clear enough for you?

ACTOR: I'm not trying to fight anybody.

MILTON: Then stop fighting. Just listen. Acting is a lot about listening. And then you respond. As a person. That's giving. Heard of it? G-I-V-E. When you look it up in a dictionary, it takes up an entire column. G-I-V-E is a lot of what makes L-I-F-E. You want to be an actor? Of course there are techniques to learn—I have a whole checklist of them. But you must give—your energy, your time, the ever-so-difficult commitment, your emotions, your heart. And when you give, it means you can then be open, and be affected by others.

Actor is getting emotional.

ACTOR: I don't know how to...I don't know what the hell you want.

MILTON: I want you to be vulnerable. I want you to let your guard down and open up.

ACTOR: Well what if I don't want to fucking open up? I don't trust you.

MILTON: Okay. I understand that.

ACTOR: I don't know if I can make it. In acting. I just don't know. *(Fighting off the emotion.)* Fuck this.

MILTON: You can make it. If you want to.

ACTOR: I want to. But maybe at the root of it I'm just not a good guy.

MILTON: You are a good guy. That's why I'm still talking. You're talented. With a lot of potential. Underneath all this bullshit is a very good guy. A romantic, even.

Actor is silent, fighting off the emotion, but tears are coming down his face.

MILTON: There you go. *(To the class:)* You see this? Beautiful. If he could do this in his acting, in his scenes— just a touch of this is all I'm after. Look how open the face is now. I'm trying to tell you all, not just him, all of you: doubts, fears and insecurity can lead to a pretended self-confidence, a kind of arrogance. The arrogance of a loser, pretending to be a winner. A kind of hostility, a chip on the shoulder. The chin cocked, ready for a fight. *(To the actor:)* Sound familiar?

ACTOR: Yeah.

MILTON: You okay, man?

ACTOR *(Wiping tears from his face):* My first day in class, someone cried in the critique, and I thought, "What total crap this is!"

Class cracks up laughing.

MILTON: You have to see this for yourself and you, only you, can then decide to end it. People who are truly confident and have self-esteem are usually pretty nice people, they can be talked to, they're charming. Can you be charming?

Actor gets up and does a soft shoe shuffle. More laughter.

MILTON: See, that's great. That's great. That's real change. A dance move like that can be a real shortcut around Charlie Freud. Remember, this is about acting. Vulnerability. Being emotional. That's what they pay big money for. So just lighten up, do that little soft shoe shuffle step. At every opportunity. Please, I beg of you, my serious, potentially gorgeous, charming friend.

The Farewell Scene

ACTOR: Before you start the critique, I just need to let you know...I'm not trying to be dramatic or whatever. But this is my farewell scene.

MILTON: What does that mean?

ACTOR: I can't do this anymore. I'm done. With class. With acting. With all of it.

MILTON: Wow. Like, finished, huh? I see. Okay. Should I still give you a critique?

ACTOR: Not really. If you want to, I guess.

MILTON: If I want to, huh? Okay. But you're leaving, so the critique would be to what end, what purpose?

ACTOR: I don't know.

MILTON: Well. I suppose I should be a professional and give you a critique. But let me ask you first: How do *you* think you did in this scene in relation to your previous work? If I said to you I was disappointed in this, would you accept it? Or do you feel there is a difference?

ACTOR: Felt like the same old thing to me, honestly.

MILTON: Same old thing. Wow. *(To class:)* And you're *sure* some of you want to teach acting?

Laughter.

ACTOR: I'm goddamned tired of this crap. I can't seem to satisfy you no matter what I do.

MILTON: Well that's okay. You're leaving. You don't have to be tired anymore.

ACTOR: Fine.

MILTON: Are we done?

ACTOR: You tell me. Nobody has ever been able to stop you from talking.

MILTON: Well, I guess I'll go on then—just to be consistent. I hope you're not too tired to hear one more thing: There's a huge difference tonight in your work. Huge.

ACTOR: Really? Or is this bullshit?

MILTON: Yeah. Really. This is the best work I've seen you do. Full. Emotional. It's like you said, "Well, it's my last scene so I might as well give everything." I think that goes in my book with about a hundred other students who have done the same thing.

ACTOR: I'm done. I'm tired. I'm tired of pushing a boulder up the mountain with this career.

MILTON: I'm sorry to hear about that. Really.

ACTOR: It's not you, though. You're not bad....

MILTON: Not bad, huh? Okay.

ACTOR: No, better than "not bad," man. Really good. But I'm done.

MILTON: I logged it. Really good. Thanks. One last thing: You have to know that what you did in this scene is what you need in your acting. Okay. That's it. I'm done. You're done. I'm done.

ACTOR: You don't have anything else to say?

MILTON: Not really. Anything you want to talk about?

ACTOR: Well, it seems kind of short.

MILTON: I'm trying to talk a little less.

ACTOR: Don't change on my account.

MILTON: Ah, c'mon.

ACTOR: No, I want to hear what you have to say.

MILTON: Really?

ACTOR: I do

MILTON: Okay, I'll tell you. When you do work like this, I take you seriously. If you could see the difference in your work tonight, the dedication, the commitment. That moment where you took her in your arms, spun her around, and really told her how you felt.... Make that part of your acting life every time out, and that would be the making of you as an actor. Your move.

ACTOR: Thanks. I hear you. But I'm up against it. I'm backed up against the wall.

MILTON: Everyone's backed up against the wall. All the time.

ACTOR: I'm too old for this shit. The business is too tough. I don't have the time. I don't have that *thing* anymore.

MILTON: That *thing*. Yeah, yeah, I understand.

ACTOR: I don't have it.

MILTON: Well, that's fine. Listen, you want the message?

ACTOR: I'm not sure. Yes. Okay.

MILTON: One of the things you hired me to do is to say when I think you're full of it. And you're full of it. About this, you're full of it. Life is hard and then you die, is that it? So what? I know the difficulty of this business. But I can't let you say to me you're coming apart, you're too tired, too old, the biz is too tough. Because I'll tell you, baby, *we're not the business*. We are not our personal problems. We are something else. Something spiritual, something unique, and something beautiful. We are leaders. If we let ourselves be crushed, we can't lead anything. We can't lead sheep to the pasture, let alone lead mankind to some kind of awareness. That's what an artist is supposed to do. Everybody has a cross to bear. And the job, the real trick of this planet, is to overcome our problems and not be swallowed up by them.

ACTOR: Swallowed up. That's how I feel.

MILTON: You're a talented actor. And if tomorrow you get a sit-com or some such thing, and all this turns around, I'm going to spit on the ground and say, "Ptooey on all that crap," because I want you to turn it all around without the sitcom. So you can say, "I'm okay with it, and I'm okay without it." And that's what I'm teaching. So, no matter what, whether you stay or you go, I wish you well.

But this class is not just learning about acting, the technical part, the craft. That's the most important, for sure, but it's also about learning and growing as a person, becoming more confident, and so developing yourself as an artist. Your acting came a long way tonight, my friend, and it's possible that you as a person aren't far behind.

Invalidation

invalidate, v., to weaken, discredit, degrade, undermine another's actions or beliefs.

A wonderful actor was a smash on Broadway a number of years ago. His name was in all the papers. Everyone was talking about this hot young actor. They said he was emotional, great with the language, fiery temperament, on and on. So people would jam the hallways after the performance, going up to his dressing room to see him, even more than went to see the big star of the show. But he did not feel the way audiences did about his work, and that's putting it mildly. Do you know what he did at the end of each performance? He left the theatre as quickly as possible by the fire escape, avoiding everyone. I directed this actor years later. In our production, he was great in rehearsals: violent, emotional, powerful. Then his wife came to town, and he weakened measurably. Obviously, they had unresolved problems. Then I thought about his Broadway story. And I felt the doubt, concern, and lack of confidence that he had from years before was still holding him back from being all that he could be. He was a good actor, but not fulfilled. Not because of lack of craft or talent, but because he had not dealt with the problem with his wife, which triggered the problem with his attitude.

Check it out. When you get a putdown, kicked in the butt by someone or yourself, check it out for these symptoms: you feel lost, dispersed, you don't want to rehearse, you get sick, you have no get-up-and-go, you have a fender-bender or you cut your finger while cooking, you hate class, your self-esteem is shot. The

bottom has fallen out for you. Definitely check it out—
this is the malaise of invalidation.

I remember during the first weeks of the run of the
original production of *Zoo Story*, which I directed, Kazan
brought Lawrence Olivier to the play. After the play,
they sent word to the stage manager to meet them at
Minetta Tavern, a restaurant near the theatre. I thought
the performance that night was terrible, I fully blamed
myself, and I was very upset. So I didn't go to the
restaurant. Brilliant! A real high mark in my life.... So
self-invalidation can be the worst. It's you doing yourself
in. It's you creating something and then, like Pac-man,
chewing it all up. It's the worst. Time and time again as
a director, I have talked with actors in rehearsal, after a
take in a film or in class—and they become Pac-man,
chewing up their work and spitting it out. Be aware of
self-invalidation as a real destroyer of what you want to
achieve. The fact is that almost always, this self-
invalidation was originated by somebody else, and you've
taken it on as your own thought. For example, some past
teacher, a real strong and authoritative type, might have
said you were the least talented student ever, and now
years later you are "invalidating yourself" by thinking
how untalented you are. So take a look at what's going on
and deal with the likelihood that someone is fucking with
you, or did so in the past in a way that is still hanging
over your head.

Step out and handle any opposition immediately. By
opposition I mean a chronic situation. I don't want to
train fragile little creatures who scream "invalidation!"
at every raised eyebrow or tiny bump from a casting
person. You've got to have a tough skin to be in this
business. But on the other hand, I've met many students

who walk out of class each week into a cesspool of chronic negativity from roommates, romantic partners, family, employers. So you need to learn to recognize this situation and figure out how to resolve it. I like to say, "I look for trouble, so that trouble doesn't find me." Resolving the matter can be as simple as a "Hey, knock it off—that doesn't help," or a more in-depth conversation (neutral ground is good—take them to lunch or coffee), and in the end, once you've really tried, and I mean *really,* you have the right to stop communicating with anyone who doesn't respond to what you need. Sometimes you discover who the person was, who gave you this wonderful invalidation. But it was long ago, and they're no longer around. They're dead. You know what I say? Go ahead and write a letter telling them what you needed. By all means, don't send it. But writing it can often bring relief.

You don't have to live with chronic invalidation. One reason you have lived with it is that it's like a fur coat against failure. You wrap yourself in it and say, "They did it. They thwarted me." Or, like some TV preachers say, "God did it." Now, I've got nothing against religion, but I don't believe God did it. He is a very busy man indeed. I believe God says, "You do it. Take responsibility and do it." And then, if anything, God might add, "Put another rock in his way. If he climbs over that one, put a bigger one in his way. Okay, good, he made it; give him a carrot—maybe a guest star spot on some new television series."

To have a career, or even to finish any movie or play, you need a Herculean effort. You need to be a pro and finish. This can't be done if you're surrounded by voices chanting *can't be done, already been done, shouldn't be* *done, they need a star name, you need an agent, they're not signing any new people, you're too young, you're too old, Uncle John was always the artist in the family—not you...*Ad infinitum. Put-downs, doubts, unsupportive comments—like weeds, they grow as long as you let them. And they don't just go away by your wishing them away. They have to be pulled up by the roots. But please, use some charm and humor. One way or the other, you must put a stop to any invalidation around you. Like St. George, slay the dragon before it opens its mouth with a fiery burp and gobbles you up.

No Buzz, No Chatter, No Jibber-Jabber

In my acting classes, the rule is nobody talks to anybody about acting or about critiques. Nobody but the teacher. It's banned. Isn't that wild? Nothing. Give them a hug or a thumbs-up if they really kicked ass, but that's enough. Leave it. Drop it. If you say more, it's more than I need as the teacher. Don't talk to the actor about his work in rehearsals, on breaks between scenes, in the parking lot after class, or over coffee that night or the next day. No consoling, no sympathy, no whispers, no nothing. And if you're standing innocently on the sidewalk during a break, and a tearful or angry actor approaches you to go off about the critique they just received—you'll do them a big favor by saying nothing, and just telling them to talk to the teacher, instead of to you. The tricky, difficult communication between a teacher and an actor is extraordinarily delicate. Same goes for the relationship between director and actor on the set and on the stage. Don't fuck with it. Don't disturb it. It should be left to the two of them. Many actors use talk about each other's work as the opening volley in a game of flirtation. I have nothing against flirtation, but titillate one other with politics, fashion, music—oh god, anything you like—but not each other's acting.

A One-Teacher Concept

Glib vs. Commitment

Fast food, fad nutritionists, fiber diets, do your own thing, cocaine, crack, pot, ecstasy, meth, pills, drive-through religion, life coaching, angst, psycho-babble, hooking up, remote control, Internet-in-your-pocket, celebrity-of-the-week, what's in, what's out, who's hip, who's not, glibness, the endless monotony of the frantic: this is the seductive fabric of today.

MILTON: What do you make of the whole teaching scene? Here you are, a young man, a kind of Jason, looking for the Golden Fleece, making your way through the world of acting. You run into one teacher, and you run into another in New York, you run into a third here in Los Angeles. And you've told me of two others you worked with. Do you think all this study is a good thing? Are you solving your acting problems?

ACTOR: Well, I think there are still a lot of areas I haven't even tapped into yet. I haven't answered your question, have I?

MILTON: No. What do you think of all these people teaching acting? You know that in this city, if you put a blindfold on, spin around a couple of times, and throw a rock, you'll hit an acting class.

ACTOR: Well, I've tried a few....

MILTON: I know! At least five! So what's going to ring the bell?

ACTOR: Well this place seems pretty good.

MILTON: Okay. It's just that in order to ring the bell, you need, and I hate this word, worse than I hate the IRS: *commitment*. People think the teacher makes the class. Not always, not exclusively. The students have a huge part in making the class. It's up to you. Otherwise, what happens is you look for the teacher to do it for you, to turn you on. You disagree, though, right?

ACTOR: Well, I tend not to get too involved in any group. Certainly the class is a group, so I kind of keep my distance.

MILTON: You can't do that. It's *your* excitement, *your* hard work, *your* upbeat attitude—that's what makes the class. Or a film set. Or a play. Individuals being enthusiastic, affecting the group as a whole. The most charismatic teacher in the world can seem powerless against the stubborn apathy of a single motherfucker in the room. Not that you're that guy....

Laughter from class.

ACTOR: Yeah. I'm weird that way—when I'm surrounded by too much enthusiasm, I just sneak out the back door....

MILTON: Is that what you're about to do here? Sneak out?

ACTOR: No, no—no way!

MILTON: Hmmmmm. Thou dost protest too much.

ACTOR: I need you, I need this class.

MILTON: I appreciate that, but I've heard it many times. And then I turn around the next week and the student is gone. And they rarely tell me directly. They tell someone else who works for me to pass it along: "I have to take a leave. I'm traveling. I've got some shit going on. I'm out of money. I'm writing a screenplay. I'm producing an indie feature." Or they tell no one. They just drop out of communication totally. I think it's about escape. The taking time off, the traveling, the no money, the screenplay writing—it's all escape. The escape seems freeing. "Wow! I have more time. I have more money. No more group enthusiasm!" The fictitious freedom to fuck up. Why are you smiling?

ACTOR: I was about to tell your class stage manager that I'm planning to take a leave of absence this summer.

MILTON: Yeah. Very few people return from these so-called "leaves." Drives me nuts. As a teacher, it's like you're playing tennis with somebody, and just as you hit this great lob, you look over the net and your opponent's racquet is just sitting there, and he's gone. And the ball just bounces to a stop. It's just not nice. It's impolite. No courtesy.

Study is difficult. I don't ever want to be in the position of having people who are glib about the study of acting. They want success, money, or as one actress said to me recently, "I want to be on billboards." I have no problem with all that. But I believe that to be there, you need to be a really fine actor. Not this thing where they just get to the point of doing good work in class and then—bang— they split. On to the next teacher. I don't understand people with six, seven, eight, twelve teachers on their resumes. This is worse than the worst Tijuana whore.

ACTOR: Well.... I had a good experience with my previous teacher. You know who that is. And I just took off. I don't really know why.

MILTON: When I have someone applying to study here, we check the situation with their previous teacher. I don't want to have someone in my class who disappeared from their previous class. We'll send applicants back to handle that, communicate with the previous teacher, resolve that honestly, before we accept them. Because otherwise we're just going to be the next class this student alienates and disappears from. So I think you should go back and handle that situation with your previous teacher.

ACTOR: I don't know if I want to do that.

MILTON: Look man, do it. It's important. Each actor should have one teacher. You should honor that teacher. And I know, I know—you look around the Beverly Hills Playhouse and see more than one teacher here. But the people who teach for me are hand-picked, personally trained, and have been here for like fifteen years, minimum. Each of them. So there's a consistency of approach. So maybe I should really say each actor should have one *teaching*. Either way, this one-teacher concept creates a powerful tool: an intimate relationship, a team, teacher and student, that focuses without compromise on the actor's work and career.

Understand, this is not about a plea for me personally as a teacher. Students come and they go—I know this, I've done this a long time. But I'm making a plea on behalf of all teachers. That they should be given their due. Their proper time to do a job. With acting, the work can be pretty extensive. If this is understood, then I believe there is a chance, a greater chance, to achieve the results that any good teacher is after. You need that commitment of time and energy with a teacher to bring about a real growth and fulfillment of your talent.

Camels

They're very thirsty....

MILTON: There's an actress in one of the classes, she always gets mixed up with screwed-up, irresponsible men. There are some men in the classes who get mixed up with screwed-up, irresponsible women. Instead of calling them screwed-up men or women, I call them camels. So, do you get involved with camels? In fact, didn't I see you driving by in Beverly Hills the other day, convertible top down, with a camel?

ACTRESS: I don't think so, but I'm not sure. I've been involved with a few camels.

MILTON: You can know them from their humps, you know, but occasionally to hide the humps they wear blazers. There are two basic types: They can be tanned from Palm Springs and Malibu, or New York pale and intense. And they spit a lot. When you see them spitting and they've got two humps, they're camels. Go the other way. You understand? And they usually smell pretty bad, camels. And, it's hard to keep a load on them. They definitely don't commit. The load keeps falling off. So when you see all those signs, you know you got a camel. Be careful. Camels have a way of blinding you and you think you might be with a zebra, or a sweet llama, or an Arabian stallion, or a big-time producer. They fool you, those stinking camels. They're deceptive. They don't look it, but they move fast, usually in a speedy Mercedes convertible—but I saw one the other day in a Volkswagon. I guess they like German cars.

ACTRESS: I'm in the process of getting rid of a camel.

MILTON: Hurry. Drop whatever you're doing and kick him out. But believe me, there's one peculiar thing about camels: As one disappears, there's another one coming over the horizon, down the freeway, over the sand dune, coming your way. It's the funniest thing. They have phones, these camels. Cell phones. Hidden in their humps, in their cars. They have e-mail. Fax. Voicemail. Internet bullshit. They contact the herd and say, "I just dropped one, so she's loose over in Bel Air. I just left her." (Camels never admit you threw them out.) "You want to pick her up? She usually goes to the watering hole over at Skybar or the Bar Marmont around eleven o'clock on Monday morning—gets a club sandwich. So sit near the window, put on that Ralph Lauren scent, and let her smell you." Is this all clear to you? If it is, watch out now, the next one's coming. I'm guessing, but is he already here? What do you think?

ACTRESS: I don't know. I'm getting away for a while. I'm going to Palm Springs.

MILTON: Oh boy, watch out! Camels love the oasis.

Certainty

Certainty is not admiration and it is not getting a job.

Certainty is not doing good work.

Certainty is not feeling good on a given day about your work, because the fact is you may not feel good about your work the next day.

Certainty is not success.

Certainty may lead to success.

Certainty is not a good review.

Certainty may lead to a good review.

Certainty is not being liked.

Certainty is not being recognized.

Certainty is not money.

Certainty is not a long-term contract.

Certainty is not applause.

Knowing one knows—that's certainty.

Certainty is certainty.

Sad Faces

MILTON: Listen, I have to tell you guys something so I can sleep tonight. There's a real shit attitude that's going on here. Right? These little piss-ant know-best cliques are forming. You feel that?

Murmured agreement from the class.

Not so much enthusiasm, please. I simply can't handle it. I want you to clean up the shit. I personally am joining the Clean Up Your Local Acting Class Mafia. I'm putting the screws to you, and making it clear that I want no more elitist cliques. This is one group, not separate groups of smart-asses. No more wandering attention. Don't sit and think of the negative things about your life, about your problems. This is no place for that stuff. We have no time for it. This is a studio for creative work. Where we all work together. I am bored with these sad, bitter faces. You are young people. Young people's faces are awful when they're bitter, sad, and disturbed. That's for older cats. Get those woeful faces out of the studio. Believe me, your professional directors won't tolerate them. They know that downbeat attitudes kill productions.

Goddamnit. I feel the rumblings, the complaints, the bitterness. I'm sick of the "I'm not booking a job" blues. Put it in a scene. Do an improvisation. Do an exercise about *geshry*-ing, which is Yiddish for bemoaning one's woeful fate. In a scene, cry. Weep. Plead to the Lord to help you. You need props to help you? Bring your Talmud, bring your crucifixes, bring your horoscopes, bring your agents. No. On second thought, don't bring your agents. These are the jokes, people. Lighten up.

Class laughter.

If you want to be here, be here. Be present and upbeat. Committed. And if you do it here, you will do it in your professional work. As I said, productions can be ruined by the negativity of just one person. So cheer the fuck up!

The Winner Gets His Critique

C'mon, man....

Two actors on stage playing a scene.

ACTOR *(In a somewhat moody fashion):* All right, I'll tell you why I'm leavin' LA. I'm leaving LA 'cause I'm sick of the scene. I'm sick of drivin' alone to a restaurant, because the person I'm having dinner with lives 10 miles in the other direction. I'm sick of hearing about some actor not having a fucking agent. Sick of every rat-infested palm tree in Beverly Hills. I want to go somewhere I never heard of—by myself. Somewhere where there's nobody who walks like you do, or talks like you do—nobody who looks like you.

ACTRESS: Scene.

Both actors sit on stage for the critique.

MILTON: Let me check something out with you. Might seem a bit weird. What is a loser?

ACTOR: A loser? I guess somebody that's got the reverse of the Midas touch: Everything turns to shit.

MILTON: Sounds pretty good. And what's a winner?

ACTOR: Well, that's Midas. That's King Midas.

MILTON: Everything the guy touches turns to gold, huh? Good. How would a winner's timing be?

Silence.

MILTON: I see. What do you think of your timing?

Pause.

ACTOR: My timing? I haven't thought about it.

MILTON: Anybody ever mention it to you, or bring the subject up?

Actor shrugs.

MILTON: Nobody in this room has ever mentioned your timing to you?

ACTOR: You mean you?

MILTON: Naaaaaah.

ACTOR: Are you saying you have?

MILTON: At least six times.

ACTOR: Then I guess I forgot.

MILTON: Let me put it to you: If a guy was paying good bread every month to get help with his acting, and the teacher told him about six times to work on his timing, and the student forgot, what would you call that guy?

No answer.

MILTON: I see. Do you think that when you're around a winner you feel good, and when you're around a loser you start to feel like your ass is dragging?

ACTOR: I don't quite know what you're getting at.

Milton rises, exploding.

MILTON: You! It's about you! Giving of yourself in the scene! Energy! Working with the other actor—moment to moment. I don't see you doing it. You're constantly letting the moment drop. You're dragging your ass. It's as if you're not there. As if you disappear.

ACTOR: I'm waiting till I know what to do.

MILTON: Don't wait! Follow your impulse. Do something. I'm tired of waiting for your waiting.

ACTOR: That's the timing....

MILTON: Timing. Energy. Giving of yourself. Why are you always standing back and measuring? Like you're measuring right fucking now while we're talking. I'm pissed off over here, and you're sitting there cool, assessing, waiting.

ACTOR: Well, you get me confused. When I'm on stage you don't think I'm giving?

MILTON: Not anywhere near what you're capable of. Why don't we come right down to it? I think you're a loser.

ACTOR: Yeah?

MILTON: I think all the arrows point in that direction. The timing. The lack of energy. Not giving of yourself.

ACTOR: You know, if you think I'm so fucking hopeless, why don't you throw me out of class?

MILTON: I was about to suggest if you don't start turning around, start understanding what's going on here, the seriousness of it, and start changing...then you can just take a walk.

ACTOR: I don't know why you're riding my ass. You're really on my case! It's as if you don't like me at all. I think you wish to Christ I'd never come around here.

MILTON: What about in other scenes you've done? Have I been shitty then, or have I encouraged you?

ACTOR: You were probably just giving me enough rope or something.

MILTON: Shit, man! The energy drops. The goddamned bottom falls out.

ACTOR: Well, if you think I'm holding this class back, I'd better get out of it.

MILTON: Is that your solution, to walk out?

ACTOR: Why not? I might just as well get the fuck out of here.

MILTON: Okay. But don't forget your stuff.

ACTOR: I won't forget a fucking thing. I'm not that much of a loser.

He grabs his stuff and walks out.

MILTON *(To the class):* See what fun teaching can be? *(To the actress in the scene:*) Why don't you tell us what you were working on.

Actor returns. Puts his stuff down and sits.

ACTOR: There's...uh...*(very uncomfortable)*...some truth in what you're saying.... But I don't know what to do.

MILTON: Let me throw something else at you. I hope it doesn't throw you any more than you already are, but what the hell. I think you're a drunk. Are you?

Another student interrupts from the class.

STUDENT: Excuse me. I have to say something. I'm really getting upset watching this because what I see is that.... Okay, I'm going to spell it out. It looks to me like you're browbeating this guy. You say he's a loser, and now he's a drunk! You've got all the power on your side and then you wonder why he's acting like someone who's powerless. He is powerless. You can kick him out anytime you want to.

MILTON: I can. But that's not what happens. Students leave on their own far more often than they're kicked out. But what ticked you off to interrupt at this particular point?

STUDENT: Because I feel like you're the big guy in this situation. The situation is unequal. You say he's a loser. We all are! No matter what he says, you're going to jab him one way or the other. How come you're so emotional about it? Maybe you're a loser, too.

MILTON: I'm trying to kill a bull here. And when I try to kill a bull, I corner him. I'm trying to kill a fucking bull here.

STUDENT: Where's the bull?

MILTON: The loser. The loser within each person in the room. Everybody who can hear what I'm saying, and yes that's including myself, has got some loser in him. That's the bull. And what you've got to do is, you corner the bull and you stick the fucking sword right down between his shoulder blades, right into the heart, and kill him. So there's no way he can escape.

STUDENT: So what's he supposed to do? Writhe and bleed to death on the floor? How's he going to get up if you destroy him?

MILTON: You destroy that loser part of him. You kill it— this loser quality that he's learned from his life, sometimes from his father, his mother, from his friends, wherever.

STUDENT: My mother doesn't happen to be my problem; it's my agent.

Class laughs.

MILTON: Don't be too sure—I've met your mother. A person should try to woo them over, convince them, bring them around, but if you can't, then yes, as tough as it is, move on. I said to my mother once, "If you love me, prove it. Undermine me once more, we don't talk ever again." And she got it. She said, "I love you, and I will change my ways." I was willing to give her up. And she changed. The whole family thanked me. *(To actor:)* So what about this drinking thing? Am I being too personal? As if I haven't been already?

ACTOR: Well, I'm not a drunk. I mean, that's crazy.

MILTON: Sorry. I was just taking a shot in the dark. You don't drink, right?

ACTOR: Well. No, I mean, I drink, but I don't drink.

MILTON: Let me ask you something. Did you have a drink before class?

No answer.

MILTON: Did you? Because you knew you had a scene to do tonight? One little one?

Beat.

ACTOR: Yes. One. I get emotional. I get upset when I'm going to do a scene. I take a drink. It knocks the edge off.

MILTON: In my opinion, for you, at this moment, that's the choice of a loser.

ACTOR: What would be better?

MILTON: This nervousness, this thing you're taking the edge off of—you've got to suffer through and let it come out. That's part of your talent. I think there's anger right on the other side of that nervousness. Hostility. And that hostility needs to make its way into your acting, not be washed down.

ACTOR: You mean I've got to play every part hostile?

MILTON: Don't be so literal. What I'm saying is you've got to take the *energy* of that hostility, and convert it into the needs of the scene. I don't need you always to be hostile when you act, but I need your point of view, your passion.

I need it expressed. I need it fucking out there, not softened, not damped down!

Actor gets up and kicks over a piece of furniture.

ACTOR: There! Does that satisfy you?

MILTON *(With explosive enthusiasm):* Yeah! That's good! Now, take the last speech of the scene, go ahead! Put this passion into that speech! Go ahead! Now, tell her why you're leaving LA!

ACTOR: You mean, you want me to do that speech?

MILTON: Goddamn it! There you go, dropping it again, measuring, waiting! Do it! Act! Now! Tell her why you're leaving LA.

Actor reads the speech with passionate intensity, blowing it out.

ACTRESS *(impressed):* Scene!

Administration

What is Administration?

Webster's:

> **administration**, n., the managing, executing, or carrying into effect of a plan; *Synonyms for administrate:* manage, control, direct, supervise, preside over.

My own definition:

> **administration**, n., the choices you make regarding the enhancement of your career and your life, and seeing to it that you complete these choices, execute them, get them *done*.

I had some really good teachers early on in my career. None of them talked about this idea of administration. University didn't talk about it, and I sure wish they had. I wish they could come up with a Life 101 course mandatory for all college seniors: It would cover credit cards, debt, real estate, some diet and health basics—like what refined sugar does to your overall health, compound interest, some basic relationship wisdom, including what alimony will do to you, plus taxes, financing a car, and career administration. You know, the stuff that actually counts.

For the actor, proactive career administration is a must. Actors famously romanticize the process—*I'll eat at this hip restaurant, or go to such-and-such a party and he'll be there—the producer, the director, Steven, Jack, Brad—he'll see me across a crowded room, remember the tape I sent him, and offer me a part right there, my career will be born....* It isn't a bad vision, it just isn't too likely. In the meantime, I prefer the saying about luck happening to people who take action. I talk about administration to get actors to be as alive, participating and knowledgeable in their careers as I've made them in their acting work.

There are plenty of bad actors out there pounding the pavement and wasting the opportunities they generate, while too many good actors—perhaps because they're more creative or more artistic and tend naturally to shy away from the business side of life—simply don't know how to get a job, or how at least to take some actions to make it more likely. Or they don't know how to audition. Or they don't get along with people. Or they're constantly in a sweat about money. Or there's some mindset that the agent or manager does this work and that's it. But anyone who's run a business knows what kind of hard work that is, and the actor is running a business: The marketing of himself and his talent in order to get work.

So once I have an actor who can demonstrate a consistent ability to act well, and who seems to have developed a good attitude—interested, open, cooperative, able to work well with people—that's when I get interested in what that actor is doing about getting work in the profession. Are they doing what is necessary to get the job? This involves a whole range of activity, including:

• being knowledgeable about what parts are being cast for what projects

• having a good relationship with your agents so you're all in agreement about what you should be reading for

• writing letters to the people you think can help move

your career forward

- visiting and befriending casting people

- writing good thank-you notes after an audition or job

- knowing about fashion and how to look good

- getting the right hair stylist

- getting your promotional tools—the reel, the website, etc.—to be really top notch

- meeting people in the industry who might be a future connection for you

- getting your ass to art galleries, concerts, studying both old and new films, exposing yourself to the other arts, cultivating a rich life

In my classes you will find that actors have formed "support groups" or "admin groups"—wherein 5-10 actors will get together once a week outside class to check on one another, if necessary to inspire and cajole one another, regarding completing actions for their career. It has been a very successful tool—it gives the students a group of peers to whom they are accountable, and they inspire one another to make the right choices for their career.

Administration also includes handling the people in your life so you have the support system an artist needs really to succeed over the long haul. Trying to deal with the parents? You know the ones—they keep comparing you to Cousin Fred in Indiana who makes $200,000 a year as a lawyer? Hard to talk to them, right? First off, check to see if you have any outstanding obligations, financial or otherwise, as this may prevent you from resolving situations with friends, family, loved ones, or even in the profession. So, for example, if you can't handle a problem with your parents, check and see if you owe them money, which makes you afraid to confront them for fear of losing financial support, or having to pay them back.

> *"Look, Mom, I don't feel you're supporting me with my acting. Now Mom, I know I owe you money. Here's what I want to do: I'm going to send you $5 a week, because that's all I can afford right now. I know it's ridiculous, because at that rate it'll take 20 years, but Mom, I need you to know that my heart's in the right place. I'm going to pay it all back. I see you don't believe me, huh? C'mom, Mom, I need your support in this...."*

Obviously, not every situation necessarily requires a conversation like this. When you're not getting encouragement as an artist from your family, that's when I would say you could apply some administration by having such a conversation. Ditto with romantic relationships. But if a friend came to see your play and has a face that makes it clear he didn't like it—well, as I mentioned before, I'm not looking to train delicate Fabergé eggs. You can't be so fragile that every speck of negativity that comes your way becomes something you need to "handle." So I'm talking about creating a balance between using a sense of administration to create a supportive environment for your continuing work and growth as an artist, and also developing a thick skin so your morale doesn't spike and dive several times a day based on a wiseass remark or passing negative comment.

"I need to talk to you about something. Now don't get upset and leave me or anything, but you never ask how my scenes go in class. It's like they don't exist for you, and I gotta tell you, it tortures the hell out of me...."

With your spouse or significant other, be aware of any fear you may have of losing their love or sexual affections. You may have a strong feeling of dependency that keeps you from wanting to confront these delicate situations. But unless you are free to handle them properly, without the fear of loss, your creative work will deteriorate.

And so this section of the book is dedicated to an actor's specific administrative needs—at least some of the issues I've seen in my decades as a teacher. It's difficult to emphasize how strongly I feel about the importance of an actor being on top of his administration, which provides for him the basis of a balanced attitude that can lead to success. Without this balance, the actor just cannot make it, because he's too overwhelmed by the problems like money, he remains worried and insecure, not knowing what to do for his career, and so tends to give up. Don't give up. Hang in there. Support and go after your dream. I've written another book, entitled *Dreams Into Action,* which was inspired by the troubles I'd observed in actors with regard to career. I suggest you look at that book as a companion to this as well. Here, however, I shall focus on some specific administrative issues, and I hope some tips will emerge that can possibly help.

Dilettante

Many years ago when I began the classes here in Los Angeles, I rented the Beverly Hills Playhouse for my use. Soon thereafter I was told that the building was up for sale, and was going to be converted to commercial space. I asked my Executive Director if the building had in fact been sold. "Yes," I was told. So I asked, "Is it in escrow?" The answer again—"Yes." My real estate broker checked—yes, it was in escrow. I said, "Check it again." He came back—yes, it was really in escrow. My reply? "No, it's not." They told me I was crazy—they had checked it, it was in escrow. I said, "No, it's not in escrow." My brother and I got a plan together and called the owner directly. I became the next owner of the building. In this instance I was not a dilettante.

So when you hear anything like....

> *"Serious? Of course I'm serious about acting. We rehearsed the scene twice!"*
>
> *"I really need a vacation."*
>
> *"The part is perfect for me, but I hear it's already cast."*
>
> *"I'm doing too many things. I'm just stressed out."*
>
> *"I don't rehearse late at night or early in the morning."*

...know that you're hearing the middle-class voice of the dilettante—killer of creativity, ally of failure, the despot of mediocrity.

dilettante, n., an amateur; one whose approach to a serious business is superficial; a person who cultivates an art or branch of knowledge as a pastime without pursuing it professionally; a person who pursues an endeavor sporadically and superficially.

My definition: A dilettante is someone who, for one justification or another, doesn't get it done; a pro does. A dilettante finds a way to escape the responsibility, and the persistence an artist has to apply in order to get the job done. It was Truffaut who said, "You start out making a movie on what you think will be the greatest adventure of your life and about three weeks into production you start to think, 'Am I going to survive this experience? Is it ever going to end?'" A dilettante doesn't finish, doesn't get the job done.

Persistent enthusiasm is a buoyant deterrent to dilettantism. Enthusiasm goes a long way in this business. As I've said before, the word enthusiasm actually means "energy from the gods." So use this godlike energy. Whether it's the drippiest television soap opera or some little play in a tiny theatre, there's only one way to do it and that's with enthusiasm. Again, attitude and administration are closely linked—this enthusiasm is the attitude with which you should go about your administration.

And remember, to get away from dilettantism, you must be precise. Don't miss even the dot on the "i," because to be a professional you don't miss a bet or a beat. The tennis pro Andre Agassi said he focused on every point. He tried his best not to let one go by, because if he let that focus go on just one point, it went away for the next two. If you deviate at all from accomplishing what you know must be done, that deviation is where you become a dilettante.

Like a bird dog, chase what you want, go after it. Don't stop because it becomes too difficult. Adversity builds character. You realize yourself in the overcoming of adversity. Most people give in to adversities, weeping and bemoaning their sad lot, lying on their paisley blanket, frustrated, furious at the unjust fate that has brought them to this moldy, depressing self-realization. That's self-pity. Tennessee Williams, in *Camino Real,* refers to this condition of self-pity as *leche mala,* spoiled milk. Self-pity has the same rank smell. The kind of self-realization I'm talking about is overcoming an obstacle; facing it, dealing with it, and changing it to your benefit. Enjoy the battle. Fight through and win. Be a warrior, not a dilettante.

In this class, you need to produce fully realized work. Some people need to stay up all night to rehearse a scene. Others need to challenge themselves with more difficult material. Still others need to do research. They need to walk up to the whore on Santa Monica Boulevard, have the guts to ask her questions and find out what a whore is all about. Or a doctor or a lawyer or a cop. Do you really want to know what a cop is like? Talk to twenty cops. And police are different in different cities. Discover the difference. It's time for all of you to break the ice and become the forerunner artists of the world. You're no longer some little guy from Pittsburgh; you're no longer the little girl from New Jersey, Texas, or California. You're not this weak character from Michigan, Vermont, Alabama. You're not your mother or your father. You're not under the influence of any of their standards, their tastes, their obligations, their limitations.

You've graduated. You're out in the world. You've got to forge your way. People like you started Cubism. Artists like yourselves started the Group Theatre, painted the Guernica, wrote *Hamlet*, built the Parthenon. People did this, artists like you. And whatever neuroses they may have possessed were bypassed or utilized to create these works of art.

So now it's time to play the game, the game of life, the game of adventure, the game of experience, the game of art. And it cannot be done if you're a dilettante. You're striving to be a professional, to be an artist. You've got to break some of the reins. And there's no such thing as can't. Get the job done one way or another, or bust yourself trying. Okay? Happy New Year!

Artistic Killer

I was interested in a new convertible car made by Volvo. I did the research on it, and found exactly what I wanted in terms of the color, the kind of interior leather, the details. I then discovered that Volvo didn't sell the 1998 convertible because of mechanical problems—they withdrew the 1998 models. This didn't stop me. Getting the number of the international president of Volvo, Mr. Johannson, in Gothenberg, Sweden, I called him. Of course, I got his secretary. I introduced myself as a film director from Hollywood, and told her that I had directed Liv Ullman, the Scandinavian actress, in *Forty Carats*.

SECRETARY: Oh, I loved that movie!

MILTON: I also spent two days with Ingrid Bergman on her island in Sweden, very near your factory.

[Speaking about Ingrid Bergman like this to a Swede is like telling an American you had lunch with Abraham Lincoln....]

SECRETARY: Isn't that nice! What can I do for you, sir?

MILTON: I want to buy a Volvo.

SECRETARY: Is there a problem?

MILTON: Yes. They won't sell me the 1998 convertible model because of certain mechanical difficulties.

SECRETARY: Oh.

MILTON: They want me to wait three months for the 1999 model—I'm not a patient man.

SECRETARY: Please hang on for a moment.

A pause ensued. A man's voice comes on the phone, and he says....

MAN: I am Mr. Johansson, International President of Volvo.

MILTON: Nice to talk to you, sir.

JOHANSSON: I am in a meeting and I don't have a lot of time, but you tell everything to my secretary and we will help you. For sure.

MILTON: Thank you very much.

The phone clicks back to the secretary, and I tell her what I want and where to reach me. Two days later, my phone rings at home....

MILTON *(gruffly)*: Hello?

MAN: Is this Mr. Katselas?

MILTON *(more gruffly)*: Yes.

MAN: My name is Ronnie Peterson.

MILTON *(most gruffly)*: What is it?

PETERSON: I am the President of Volvo North America.

MILTON *(sweet as butter)*: Hello, sir! So nice of you to call.

PETERSON: I just spoke to Mr. Johansson in Gothenberg, and I said to myself, I must speak to this man.

MILTON: So very nice of you.

PETERSON: You know, I can't sell you a 1998 convertible because the company has withdrawn them.

MILTON: I know. But I'm not the most patient man.

PETERSON: I know, I know. Mr. Johannson's secretary told me.

MILTON: Oh.

PETERSON: I can't sell you a '98 right now. But I have a convertible '98 of my own on which we fixed the mechanical problem, and I am going to give it to you.

MILTON: Well isn't that nice of you! What do you mean "give"?

PETERSON: You can use it until the 1999 model comes out.

MILTON: That's awfully nice. What's the charge?

PETERSON: Oh, no charge at all.

MILTON: Very nice of you. There is one more thing. My 1999, when I order it, I want the bigger engine that you put into the coupe. Could that happen, as a special thing?

PETERSON: A man like you can get anything he wants.

Five days later, Mr. Peterson's car arrived as he said, washed and fully gassed. I drove it for six weeks and then returned it. My own Volvo, with the special engine, arrived very soon thereafter, one of best cars I've ever owned—I am grateful to that gracious Swedish company.

So why this story? Why is this chapter called "Artistic Killer?" By Artistic Killer I mean someone who finishes what they start, someone who leaves no stone unturned in trying to get a job done. I mean a focused, energized, hardworking professional who never takes no for an answer. An Artistic Killer embodies the fusion between attitude, the feeling with which you do something, and administration—the choices you make, then getting these choices done no matter what. As you are doing a specific project, believe you can do it. Know that you'll get it done. Continue the actions towards getting it done. Don't wait. Don't hesitate. All of this is necessary to finish the job.

I'm reminded of my parents, who were very religious, and who at least twice each year helped to promote a bazaar to raise funds for their church. Their mission was clear and defined. They were passionate and determined because to them this work was God's work, and so they were more than determined in going after their goal of how much money was to be raised by what time. They called people, wrote to them, visited candy stores, restaurants, hotels, garages, hospitals, dress shops, shoe repair shops, you name it. And may God protect those who said no, for if my parents were rejected they still went back a second and even a third time, each time a little more aggressively. I remember the heated discussions in the kitchen with our priest, determining who to go to next, and constantly appraising how much they had raised so far, and what else they needed to do to achieve their goal.

It is difficult to describe the zeal with which my parents went after their target. "We're going to make god-fearing people out of these cheapskates!" It was a kind of almost bloodthirsty, humorous, fun attitude, trying to develop plans to solicit money from their various prey. And the quest to achieve the set goal did not end. At the bazaar itself, they created an auction, having received donations of many items to be bid on at the bazaar. The head auctioneer was primed, coached and jazzed up by my parents, so that he was in top form, selling his wares with great energy and humor. They also sold tickets before the bazaar for a kind of lottery, and continued to sell tickets up to the selection of the winner.

Then everyone would dance, and a basket was placed in the center of the dance floor, into which contributions were placed to celebrate the most exciting, skilled dancers. Then my mother danced. Look out, man, she really strutted her stuff—no moves barred. It was a sexy, impassioned dance that drew everyone's attention and filled at least two baskets. And after the bazaar, my parents continued with their fundraising, never stopping, for besides their family, nothing was more dear to them than the church. They were real people with an attitude of love and passionate desire.

In this avenue of fundraising for the church and in the Volvo adventure, there is clearly the concept of what I mean by Artistic Killer: someone who uses constructive actions to complete, or kill the deal that they are after ("kill" meaning to complete to the fullest, most productive degree). So an actor can increase his Artistic

Killer quotient by really chasing a character—doing the
research, rehearsing like mad, nailing the accent, really
pushing with some zeal the envelope of their acting
work. An Artistic Killer actor doesn't take no for an
answer about an audition. You want to read for that
part? Find the producer. Find the director. Write a killer
letter. Get in there. Prepare your audition to your very
best and more—keep yourself in top form in class by
giving your all, make sure you're physically and
emotionally ready to go. Trouble paying for class? Second
job. Better first job. Work at night. Clean the theatre.
Mr. Kazan's first job was to sweep up the space for the
Group Theatre. Get it done, and continue to pursue your
administration with zeal and a sense of fun. Artistic
Killer can be considered an attitude—a certain no-holds
barred enthusiasm and determination—but is primarily
someone who makes the proper choices and gets them
done, and so has killer administration. You must believe,
you must care, you must never accept no, you must
persist, and you can accomplish your goal no matter
what obstacles present themselves. Whether you're
competing with better known actors, or the part is
against your type, or they aren't seeing anyone—you
make the moves to get the audition and show them what
you can do. Remember, thay say it's not over until the fat
lady sings—well there is no fat lady and she doesn't sing
anyhow. It's only over when *you* say it's over.

Casting

A constant headache-creating piece of anguish. Worse than taxes. Worse than sex. Oh, yes. It is the Grim Reaper. This horror for the actor, simply stated in a word, is: *casting*. How do I get this part? What part should I do? How do I get better parts? How do I get parts for which they never think of me? The classic: *What's my casting?* How do I get any part at all? How? How? How? It's a subject that often brings the onward rush of the actor's career to a sputtering, clanking, I'm-never-gonna-work-again halt. Nightmarish or not, being knowledgeable about casting is part of your acting technique. The understanding of your casting, and being able to execute it, is a big part of the whole equation. If you don't think so, put Lawrence Olivier in *High Noon* and let Gary Cooper play *Richard III.*

First off, look at movies, television, plays. But keep in mind you're no longer a civilian spectator, just enjoying the ride. As you watch a movie, find your part. Be honest. And don't be greedy. Pick the part that's right, that you can play, that you could be cast in for real—not the lead role every time. Maybe there's a one-scene part for a lawyer and you're good at lawyers. Pick that part and do it in class so you feel you're as good as you can be, and you can honestly compete for this role. Get real. Get clear. This is part of administration. I love dreams, but I want doable dreams.

A longtime student went on this casting trip in class with me where all she wanted to play were romantic leading roles, á la Joan Crawford. But this was a character actress, a down-to-earth woman who could easily play the common folk. We went back and forth—she fought me over this issue. Finally, she gave in. Now, years later, it seems almost every other movie I see, she's in it, playing interesting character parts. She finally realized her casting and started working professionally nonstop.

Acting is extremely personal—it's you. To look at the issue of casting is not about invalidating your personality or your physicality or your dreams. I don't want you thinking to yourself, "I'm too big/small/old/young/tall/short/pretty/not pretty, etc., to play that role." No. It's about understanding in a simple, direct way what roles you're currently right for, those roles that fit you like a glove, what I sometimes refer to as the "first circle" of casting. The role that the actor can just step into with little effort. You need to know what your first circle is, and recognize that industry people will probably see you a certain way at first. Once you understand that, accept it, and you've nailed these parts in class, then go for that dream role you've always had in mind to play.

A Korean-American actress in my class was, early on, very uptight about being cast only as an Asian. She was really waving a flag for race-blind casting, and it was sometimes just a bit much. When we thought of scenes where she would play an Asian part, she rolled her eyes. Then, she was asked to play a waitress in a Chinese restaurant in a scene in class. She decided to play it as the epitome of the stereotypical owner of a Chinese restaurant. You know what happened? She was hilarious. She was a scream. She stole this scene so thoroughly.... Then she played the lady whose purse was snatched in *Detective Story* as a Korean immigrant with terrible English—brilliant. Within a year after that, she had developed an entire comedy act about a Korean immigrant who wants to be a standup comedian, speaking in horribly broken English, who only knows the corniest and most insulting race jokes. The act won a bunch of awards, big ones. And then she booked television roles. Yeah, some were cliche Asian roles, but also some that were not specifically Asian. But she works all the time. This is what I mean about finding your first circle and having some humor about it all.

But as is often the case with acting—there's another story, another angle on it. Because I don't want to pigeon-hole you in this first circle. I have often found that when an actor tries out those "stretch parts," the ones that are actually *away* from that first circle—this can often be an important moment in training. I assign the blue-collar guy who never went to college to play a fancy lawyer. I force the character actress to be the femme fatale, like in *Fatal Attraction.* It's an interesting deal—you give them permission to explore a whole different area of their talent, and that exploration tends to affect the first circle positively as well.

When you audition, understand they have a problem: They have to cast this part. So walk in with the idea that they don't have to look anymore. You are the ticket. Through your audition, let them know, "I'm it. I'm the answer." Some actors bring a bunch of apology into their auditions. It's as if they're apologizing for being there. A doctor I know, meeting a friend of mine for the first time, said as he was examining him, "Why don't you stop apologizing for the fact that your father is a bricklayer?" You want to know something funny? His father was a bricklayer. It was so ingrained in my friend's behavior and attitude, that it was quite readable to someone with a bit of perception.

You can't be limited by the idea of where you came from, or what your parents were like, all that baggage. You have to move beyond your past. If you don't, and you allow yourself to feel a certain shame about it, or the reverse, like a stubborn pride that prevents you from, say, dressing well for certain roles, or just looking your best in general, it can create a feeling of negativity that isn't true to who you really are. You're an artist. You have talent. You have imagination. You have to go beyond the *mishegas,* the negative thoughts that you've held knowingly or unknowingly. So, if you're apologizing because of your family, or your looks, talent, or lack of education, realize that it shows, it's oozing all over the place, and people are picking up on it. This is where attitude hits you as you try to do your administration with regard to casting. You're an actor. Make choices that move you beyond your limited conception of yourself. I once bought an Armani suit that I couldn't really afford because I loved the way it made me feel— you sometimes need to give yourself a little jolt in life to break out of the box you may have put yourself in, and you have to do it in your acting as well.

Remember in school when you had a substitute teacher? The substitute, a little weaker in skill, and seeking to be liked, didn't command your attention or respect. Well, don't send in a substitute actor for yourself, a weak, ineffectual, mousy, ingratiating actor, so all they see is this apology. They may not know why, but they don't hire you.

By the way, sometimes beautiful people apologize because they're attractive. Weird, huh? They come to class and try to look unattractive. "I'm not attractive. Please, don't think that I'm handsome or beautiful, because that means I'm not talented." The world has a prejudice that handsome, beautiful people are not talented. When Robert Redford first appeared on Broadway, we, the splendid *cogniscenti*, the smart-asses, thought, "He's that handsome? And talented? No way." Or they hide their beauty or handsomeness because they're trying to avoid unwanted attention. No good. They're apologizing for the very radiance that may be a key part of their casting. They make this a habitual way of behaving and being. They may think, "Oh, I'll just turn it all on tomorrow at 2 p.m. for my audition." I don't think so. The hiding becomes a habit that bleeds into the acting, and the auditions.

As I mentioned before, Cary Grant spoke to the classes here and said, "All you have is you." So bring all of you to the party, each time. As if you're saying to the audience, *"It goes like this, folks. Watch me. This is how it's done."* No apology.

I remember directing *After The Fall*. I had Jose Ferrer in the lead role, and was desperately, for weeks, looking to cast Maggie. The word was out that we were frantic. Then one day, while casting in a place near 50th Street in New York, in walked Karen Black. And she said quite simply, "You don't have to look anymore." Those were the first words out of her mouth. I asked if she could sing, and she dropped the books in her hands and broke out singing. Then I had her read about two lines of the first scene, and that was it. I gave her the part on the spot. She did it. And she did a great job. Your talent needs to be backed up by certainty and a sense of humor. It doesn't mean you'll get the job, but it sure does help to present yourself as the solution to their problem.

I'm Looking To See If I'm Talking To A Human Being— Not An Actor

Interviews with Milton

MILTON: One of the most exciting things in our business is the discovery of a new talent, and the search is constant. All the great directors have been interested in new people, new faces.

QUESTION: How does one get there to be discovered? Does luck play any part? For instance, some people may work hard, be extremely talented, and not be in the right place at the right time.

MILTON: I don't believe that luck plays any part. "Luck happens to people of action who are ready to capitalize on the opportunity that happens to them." That's from *The Richest Man in Babylon.* Every person has a different road to take and some people are discovered quickly and easily. Others have to persist. Timing, you might say, is part of it. An actor hears about something, immediately tells his agent, and gets in the running for the part. The actor does what he can to get the audition. When he gets it, then it's up to his talent. If I thought luck was the determining factor, I'd pack my bags and head for another planet.

QUESTION: Does the actor wanting to work professionally in film and television require training in legitimate theatre?

MILTON: Acting in a play and creating, in two-and-a-half hours, the whole performance in one piece takes discipline and control. Eight shows a week of that and the actor really crawls into the skin of the character. This definitely helps the actor in film work, because you're often shooting out of sequence, but need always to be aware of the character, and the relationship of each scene to the story as a whole. You get that in the theatre, when you have to do it all in one piece, and you really get some time with it.

QUESTION: When you are casting a film and someone comes in for an audition or meeting, what, if anything, sparks you?

MILTON: Painters, sculptors, musicians create through canvas, clay, musical instruments, so we are not as concerned with what personal attributes emanate from them. When the actor walks on stage, without even doing any acting, certain qualities emanate from him. He is the creator and the created. As the director, you have a mental picture of what you want for each role, and that picture is not just physical, but it's also a picture of a very specific emotional range and the kind of person you want for the part. Basically, I'm trying to see what this person is like: humor, intelligence, personality. Another thing: Can this person be a part of a group project? Can we live and work together for what is sometimes three or four months or more?

QUESTION: If you were a young actor starting out, what would be your course of action? What would you do?

MILTON: First off I'd get myself a nice, healthy place to live—safe and bright. Then get myself a good acting teacher, voice coach, dance, gymnastic training. Also, though, the actor has to devise his own plan and follow his own course. For example, when I was an actor and graduated from Carnegie Mellon, I said to the head of the drama department that a week after I moved to New York I was going to be studying acting with Lee Strasberg and working for Elia Kazan. He was highly skeptical. But I had a plan. That first week, I was walking in the street and there was Elia Kazan. I chased him, went up to him and spoke Greek, we got along and I started working for him. At the same time, I started Strasberg's acting class. You have to decide, have to have a plan of action and carry out that plan. You can't just sit there and wait, can't put yourself on hold.

The apprentice system in Europe is still very important and I am amazed that more people don't take advantage of it here. In my first year in New York I apprenticed for Kazan, Josh Logan, Joe Anthony and Sanford Meisner. I learned more in that period about acting and casting and what makes a real Broadway show than I did in four years at school. There are many stories of actors who have become "gofers" (go for this, go for that) for directors, and suddenly they're put in the film or the play. The only route not to go is the no route way, just sitting back and thinking, "They'll call me." That doesn't work.

QUESTION: Do you feel that some acting classes can squash that special quality that one might have, take away an originality, a uniqueness?

MILTON: I can see the acting teacher who might tell Humphrey Bogart that he has bad speech and needs to correct it. So actors have to be alert, but they shouldn't be overly cautious about entering a class, you cannot think, "I can't go into this situation because I might get burned, I might get hurt." You have to throw the dice, commit and give of yourself. And you won't know just from one class. That's why I don't allow auditing of my classes. A good restaurant reviewer will have several meals at a place before writing the review. Students who come to my class pay for eight weeks up front, because I think it takes at least that long to really assess the teacher, the students, the vibe, the sensibility of a class, and to see honestly if it will help you.

QUESTION: Do you think that success is also a question of finally getting the right part—the part that will show off an actor and his or her specific gifts at the right time?

MILTON: Well, that's part of it, but more interesting to me is what led an actor to get that role. It's about a change within the actor. A change occurred in the attitude toward their work; they met some teacher, they met some director, something very profound happened which changed them and provided the juice. When Geraldine Page did *Summer and Smoke,* or Jason Robards got *The Iceman Cometh,* those were roles that came at the exact right time, both directed by the excellent Jose Quintero, who used the right qualities of both those actors, and really put them on the map and allowed them to be recognized as terrific actors.

QUESTION: In terms of the casting process, you are a great one for pushing the responsibility onto the actor: "Go read the material. What part would you like to play?"

ACTING CLASS

MILTON: I don't like the actor to feel as if he's just told what to do or what role to play. I want to hear what the actor thinks. Eventually the responsibility for the role is going to be more in the hands of the actor than the director. In the beginning, the director knows more about the role than the actor, but eventually the actor knows more. I got that from Harold Clurman. In the theatre, on opening night the director is either nervously pacing the theatre or is drunk in a nearby bar. It's the actor who is on stage, facing the critics and the audience. They say film is a director's medium. Ever seen a great film with bad acting? So I'm always trying to get the actor to be more and more causative.

QUESTION: What about the issue of working actors who get locked into a certain casting, so they're only seen in a very limited way by the industry?

MILTON: If you are a working actor and want new, better, or different roles, don't just complain or dream about it, but really nail what you want and deliver it in a class. I know it's easy for a working actor to get pigeon-holed into a certain kind of role—but this can be changed. Let the people with whom you have worked in the past know of your new found desires and abilities. Write them a letter, give a call, really let them know. Invite them to see your work. That's what I call administration. Read for the parts they gave you before and also ask to read for that other role in the script that you want. If you're convinced, that will help to convince others. As always, try to be courteous about all this—the people whose minds you need to change will probably respond more to a polite charm than a frantic intensity.

QUESTION: Any last words of advice?

MILTON: An actor should have a sense of dignity. And by dignity, I don't mean pride, I don't mean hostility. I mean a sense of dignity, an awareness that he is in one of the most influential of all professions. Maybe an actor has difficulty qualifying for a mortgage, but that's not what I'm talking about. I'm talking about dignity in the sense that the actor knows that through his creativity he can affect people in the most profound ways. An actor can do this. That's his dignity.

So, when an actor goes for an audition, he doesn't have to be a beggar who says, "I've got to have this job." No matter how broke he is, he must not be talked out of that dignity, no matter what. Through his work, an actor can illuminate and affect the day-by-day lives of people, and their relationships and their dreams. In the real attempt to be a person, to have dignity, there is no promise of absolute success, but this kind of attitude will be a definite presence in the interview or audition. His presence will help him connect with his talent and give a truer picture of his abilities.

This material was adapted from interviews with Milton in How To Make It In Hollywood by Wende Hyland and Roberta Haynes, and How To Audition by Gordon Hunt.

Drugs And Alcohol

You're not Toulouse-Lautrec

Speed, right into the vein. Not with pills, just straight up. No sleep for seventy-two hours and you begin to feel like you could rule the world. Then one morning, in the same mood where I thought I could rule the world, I couldn't tie my own shoelaces. And at that moment, oddly enough, I also recognized that my life, my energy, was in this little vial of methamphetamine. This little vial was responsible for how good I was going to be that day, not me.

That morning I realized that the little vial on the nightstand, which was the first thing I focused on, was not me. I felt a separation from it and a sense that I was waiting on this little vial to provide my juice, to supply my energy to face the day, and that this little vial was never consistent. The hit I got in the morning was totally different from the hit I got at night. Same little vial. So in those few seconds I concluded: that's it, no more, and I began to gradually slide off. In a month, I was totally clean. So you see, this point of view comes from someone who has been there and knows firsthand why people make these kinds of choices, why they feel they need this kind of false lift, which then becomes a whole way of life.

I believe one reason for this drug and booze way of life is a desire for fantasy, escape from boredom and apathy. The hum-drum everyday activity is falsely relieved by the exciting activities connected to finding the source for drugs, negotiating for drugs, administering the drugs, experiencing the drugs, the dangers and problems with your dealer or doctor. The drug user feels like a very busy man indeed. His real problems seem far away. All this is a phony substitute, done to avoid the reality of life. Now the same thing happens with booze. An alcoholic told me once that booze softened everything visually and emotionally. That's why she liked the soft light at the end of the day—what cinematographers call "the magic hour." This softening made life easier to swallow. Behind this, of course, was the fear of knowing the truth, the fear of life as it is.

One of the many big problems with drug use is that it's impossible to predict the results. Anybody who tells you that you can know the answer, a predictable answer of what happens to you when you take drugs, is off his rocker. You can never really know, even from hit to hit. I'm talking about booze, I'm talking about marijuana, I'm talking about hash, I'm talking about speed, I'm talking about cocaine, I'm talking about ecstasy, meth, diet pills, antidepressants, sleep-disorder medications, Valium and other prescription drugs. Yes, even over-the-counter stuff.

I'm not talking right now about the detrimental effects on your health or your brain, though the scorecard is plain on these counts. I am talking about inconsistent results in your art. So your work, your creativity become subject to unpredictability. You want results that are predictable and you want to be certain your acting craft is the reason for what is expressed in performance, and not some lucky high.

As far as work in class, I don't think anyone should have any alcohol or other drugs (street, prescription, or over-the-counter) for a minimum of twenty-four hours before class. I'd like to be stronger about it, but the rest is up to you. It's a known medical fact, by the way, that these drugs can take weeks to leave your system. Marijuana, for instance, takes about four weeks to get where there's no residue left to lessen the user's reaction time. There's also the factor that users will need an increased amount of the drug to get the sensation they want, to keep the action going. But no matter what you say about it, the bottom line is no one should come to professional work or the class while high on booze or drugs.

And in case you're thinking, "Hey, such-and-such an actor is a user and he does really well, and Toulouse-Lautrec took absinthe and look what he accomplished!" I've got some news for you: The only way you could ever do what Lautrec did is to become 4' 8" tall, go to Paris, live his life, feel alone, paint the women he painted, fall in love with a whore, and take absinthe, and hope that all equations come out equal. You can't trade your equation with anyone, and besides, Lautrec came to a tragic end at the age of thirty-seven, a victim of alcoholism. So much for that romantic view of Paris.

"Well, okay, Milton, you had your sensations, what about ours?" The point is, if I had it to do again, I wouldn't. There are no regrets connected with my actions of the past, but it was truly of no real value to me, and led directly to my mishandling two jobs and being fired from one.

So let me hear from you on this subject. You're not going to be booted out, you're not going to be chastised. If I know where you're coming from, there'll be no lies between us. It will all be out in the open. I've shared with you my viewpoint, and what you do about it will be what you do about it.

Commissary Talk

MILTON *(taking out a piece of paper)*: I was up late last night and made some notes here—I wanted to read them to you, might be of some interest:

Heard, on the corner of Beverly and Orlando: *You aren't still in that acting class, are you?*

Laughter from the class.

MILTON: I guess that hits the mark. Let me read more:

Meanwhile, at Sony: *Who's your agent?*
                              I'm with Dan Smith.
                              Oh.... (odd silence)

And at Culver Studios: *You're reading for Kathy tomorrow? Ten bucks says she doesn't smile the whole time you're in the room.*

And at Paramount: *I don't want to spread a rumor, but our producer looks as if he could use a trip to Betty Ford....*

On location: *He doesn't seem quite in top form, does he? It's because his wife just left him....*

In the dressing rooms everywhere: *Did you agree with the note the director just gave you? Because I thought you were great.*

More laughter from class, as Milton puts away the paper.

MILTON: Ah, the many virtues of friendly, sharply-targeted talk in the commissary on a lunch or dinner break. The fun, the joy and the sweet relish that you feel as you tear apart your writer, producer, fellow actor or director! Isn't it delicious as you see someone's body and reputation bite the dust—oh so nutritious, oh so delicious! By pushing commissary talk, you are rising to the true glory of man's best achievements!

No. Don't do it. Stop. Please. Commissary talk sucks. And understand, this is a choice. You choose to do it, or you choose not to. It's in your hands. You all heard of a filmmaker named Francis Ford Coppola?

An amused affirmation from the class.

MILTON: Yeah, he's done a couple of small films. He said, "Never talk against another filmmaker." That's him. That's what I'm talking about.

I'm trying to encourage a kind of social revolution within this business. I believe you can lead that revolution, that you personally can change the nature of the sets and theatres where you work. We need to make every effort to destroy commissary talk in our profession, at every sound stage and in every theatre, in every makeup trailer, in the coffee shops near the rehearsal halls, maybe broaden it out to the swank bistros of L.A., definitely we need to kill it in the acting classes and the cheap diners where hip banter and casual gossip are every day destroying creativity, disempowering people, and flushing projects down the toilet. I know this sounds harsh, but how many of you have been in a production that was hurt by negative gossip?

Class response.

You bet. I'm not interested in wasting your time with a philosophical pursuit driven by some Utopian notion of "love for your fellow man" or something. Love for your fellow man is great, but ultimately I'm interested in acting, in creating effective actors. Effective actors make good choices, smart choices—in their work and in their lives. Good choices that are carried out. That's what administration is about. I think commissary talk sucks because the person it hurts most is you. The place it hits you hardest is in your paycheck. It hits you hard because you're tearing down the very thing you're trying to build, whether it's your play or your movie or your class. And that's completely irrational.

The intent of commissary talk is to take someone down, reduce them, in a sense erase them. The effort to destroy them is in part to make you seem stronger—commissary talk is fraught with jealousy and envy. It can occur through an outright negative remark or through subtler means. Facial expressions, eye rolls, deep sighs, and ominous silences can be the foot soldiers that lead to fullblown destructive attacks. Commissary talk lingers and can poison your relationships and the projects you're involved in.

The most commissary talk gets you is temporary membership to a club whose natter and chatter are doing nothing to improve conditions in this world. And trust me, your membership is temporary because a major part of the sickness of commissary talk is that if today you and the gang are badmouthing Joe, then tomorrow Joe and the gang are badmouthing you.

If you want your television pilot or waiver play or big movie to be successful, you must protect your peers, protect your crew, protect your top people from attack. Keep them strong. Especially those at the top. If they get attacked and weakened it'll be a real mess. And because they're running the show, it won't just be a mess for them, it will be a mess for everybody on the project. You understand this?

CLASS: Yes!

MILTON: So how do you handle commissary talk when it comes to you? Cut it off! Personally, I won't tolerate it. I tell people to stop it, as I am telling you. I embarrass them. I give them an icy-cold fucking stare. I ask all sorts of annoying questions, like "Who exactly said that?" "What do you mean exactly?" "Why don't you handle that?" "Why are you making trouble?" Or, "How about you and I handle this negativity right now?" It all becomes very unpleasant for the commissary talkers, and they tend to stay away from me. So don't flinch and walk away, telling yourself you're unaffected and it's none of your business. It is your business. Fix it. See that it gets fixed. Be a leader. Be a mensch. Listen to Coppola. Knock it off.

Money Is Real

So here goes: Another not-ever-talked-about, touchy, unusual area for perusal by an acting teacher. But then again, I'm sure I'm not the only teacher who, upon asking after a student who is missing from class, hears in response an endless litany of financial issues that keep said student from affording tuition. And tuition is sometimes the least of it—the same student is driving without insurance, has overdue parking tickets, an irate landlord, unpaid credit cards, *etc., ad nauseum.* The issue of financial responsibility seems to hit the artist at all points during his or her career, which can certainly have its boom and bust cycles.

My belief is that money is a resource to be managed with simple, real, practical actions. You assess your income, set up a budget listed by priorities, keep to this budget in a disciplined fashion, and proceed. No shopping sprees, no clubbing, no expensive restaurant binges. Keep an eye on your cash layouts. I have found that students struggling to pay for class will spend $10 or more a day on little purchases like coffee, magazines, and sweets. That's upwards of $300 a month. Credit card debt—wow, is this prevalent! But even five-digit credit card debt can be handled. The first step is just to stop using the damned things. Use ATM debit cards instead, the kind that take your purchase directly from your checking account, instead of a credit card you inevitably avoid paying off. And if you're paying exorbitant interest, you can restructure the debt at a lower rate, consolidate it so you have one payment—easier to pay off.

But here's the number one simple change you can make to change your financial life forever. Ready? *Save ten percent of any income before you do anything else. And then never, ever, ever touch it.* Did you receive a check for $100? Put $10 away first. Did you make $50 in tips last night? Put $5 in an envelope and get it to the bank. You should do this *regardless of debt, regardless of what bills are unpaid.* You do this first, pay yourself first, then deal with the mess that is left.

This puts me at odds with those who say you should tackle high-interest debt before you start saving. They're right about the math of it, but I disagree because the savings is about you, it's about your future, it's about saying your future starts right now, regardless of the current situation. And don't touch the savings. Ever. Later on you can *move* it somewhere, to an asset, a building, a business, something that makes more money for you. But never ever withdraw from your savings to handle an expense or bill or debt, or to "celebrate" by buying something you can't really afford. Because then you'll constantly be starting all over again.

This 10% savings is not a rainy day fund. If you want a rainy day fund, that's another 10%. The first 10% is your "Someday I want a life where I don't worry about my day-to-day expenses and I can focus on my art and my acting and what-I-like-to-do fund." Disciplined savings is not about scarcity, about endless sacrifice. Life is full of many things that can enrich us, educate us, inspire us, make us happy. So if you, every once in a while, come across something that does this in some way, a painting, or an old Jaguar, as I did when I was younger, well, I got them. I increased my debts by doing so. But then I worked my ass off to earn more, and I didn't take the purchase out of my savings. Your level of debt may go up and down, but the savings you simply do not touch.

Discipline is the key. Saving 10% off the top will get things rolling, but you still have to work hard. If you need more money, find a day job that doesn't interfere with your auditions or rehearsals, or deplete your energy. As a young man in New York, I had a job on a moving truck—we worked the first four days and the last four days of each month, when people did all their moving. The rest of the time I was free. This is causative action, where you take the responsibility rather than being a victim of circumstance. Life is real. Money is real. There is nothing mystical or magical or awesome about financial responsibility. An excellent book to read about handling money is *The Richest Man in Babylon*.

The Warrior (Guerrero)

A Warrior leaps into battle.

A Warrior adopts aggressiveness as a stance towards life that rouses, energizes, and motivates.

A Warrior is not stuck with one way. He is flexible, using razor-sharp evaluation.

A Warrior is constantly improving communication skills.

A Warrior never holds a grudge.

A Warrior fully understands celebration.

A Warrior knows every act counts.

A Warrior doesn't think too much. Thinking leads to doubt, doubt to hesitation, hesitation to inaction, inaction to losing.

A Warrior can comply easily and freely to someone else's orders—and his own. Someone told me once that you'll never be able to direct unless you're willing to be directed.

A Warrior doesn't try to be right, he just fixes things in his working and personal relationships.

A Warrior is definitely the guy who walks through the threshold, if the threshold needs walking through.

A Warrior follows Kazan's idea that 80% of being an artist is the ability to get along with people.

A Warrior is willing to confront. Or not. By his own decision.

A Warrior is a pro. He gets things done. Now.

A Warrior does not even know how to spell flinch.

A Warrior is energetic, decisive, courageous, enduring, persevering, and loyal to some greater good beyond himself. And he can be humorous.

A Warrior will only destroy what needs to be destroyed so that something more valuable, more effective can appear.

A Warrior masters the techniques of his craft—and his life—through continuous study, discipline and stretching the boundaries.

Roulette

ACTOR: I have a question about what you've been saying about casting. I like the part about an actor having dignity. But my thing is like, you're an actor and you hear of a project happening, and you say, "Yeah. Yeah, that's right for me. I could possibly do that." Then the director, in this case you, uses so many finite details and decisions, whether to use the actor or not for a specific part, that I say, "Wow, man! You know? Like, if I part my hair differently from what the director has envisioned in his head, I'm out."

MILTON: Or in.

ACTOR: Or in. Right.

MILTON: What else?

ACTOR: I guess what I'm saying is that I feel an actor, no matter how much dignity he maintains, has very little influence on the ultimate casting decision—you know, roulette.

MILTON: Who makes the decision?

ACTOR: The director. And the people who are creating the project.

MILTON: I see. You think they make their decisions alone in the office.

ACTOR: Before the office, even.

MILTON: So you're saying an actor can't really go out and get the part, because it really isn't up to him?

ACTOR: Well, yeah. We're almost helpless. We have so little power over anything.

MILTON: Sure. Like Robert Redford, Dustin Hoffman, Marlon Brando, Julia Roberts, Vanessa Redgrave. No power, they're all just victims.

ACTOR: Yeah, but they're stars, and we're just no-name actors.

MILTON: Those stars were "no-name" actors at one time. You don't come out of the womb a "name." Well, maybe Drew Barrymore....

Laughter.

ACTOR: It seems that the choice is so dependent on the director's concept of what the part is.

MILTON: The real point of the matter is that the actor, whether no-name or name, can convince the director, the producer, even though their image of the part is totally different. Take *The Graduate*, which was cast by my friend Mike Shurtleff. He said they went looking for blond guys, Ivy League types, six feet tall, and they ended up with Dustin Hoffman. Because of his talent, they changed the whole image of the character. And Dustin wasn't very famous at that time, not a star, he wasn't *Dustin Hoffman* yet by any stretch.

ACTOR: Okay. That's one.

MILTON: *Butterflies Are Free:* I cast a guy who had never acted before, Edward Albert, who, when he heard about this film, told his father, "I'm going to play the lead in that movie." Now you can't say that my concept was a guy who had never acted before. But as he read for us, there was no denying that he was the part—he defined the concept for us.

ACTOR: Uh huh. Okay, two.

MILTON: My friend, I can go to 100 and beyond. In casting the play, *Streamers*, an actor from class, Richard Lawson, worked on a reading for the part. He told me, "I'm going to get that part. I mean, that's it. No question. It's mine." He fully committed himself to the reading. No holds barred. During the reading with Richard Thomas, who was already cast, Lawson pulled a switchblade and scared the shit out of us. The producer was like, "Who the hell was *that* guy?!" I pretended I'd never seen him before. We couldn't conceive of anyone else after that. He was truly excellent in the role.

ACTOR: But all those little tests to see if the actor is right for the project—it always sends a chill down my back.

MILTON: Well, what's the matter with you? Are you flawed?

ACTOR: Am I flawed?

MILTON: Yeah. Is there something the matter with you that we're going to find out? Why wouldn't every test confirm your rightness more and more?

ACTOR: Oh, just...uh...I just assume that whatever the director's concept is for the part, I'm not it.

MILTON: That's the whole problem. Okay. Let's solve it. If I hold a concept of the part as a director....

ACTOR: ...then I don't get the job.

Class laughs.

MILTON: You're joking, but that's what you really think. Are you sure it's alright with you if I have a concept at all?

ACTOR: I'd rather you didn't, honestly.

MILTON: Why would you rather I didn't?

ACTOR: Because I'm the actor. I'm bringing the concept to the part.

MILTON: That's great. I like an actor who brings a concept. Couldn't your concept be just as good as mine? Or better?

ACTOR: Sure. I mean, I think I should have the role. That's how much I believe in my concept.

MILTON: So how are you going to let me know about that concept?

ACTOR: Show you. I'm going to read for you. Audition.

STUDENT (*From the audience*): Milton, can I say something about this? Just because it hits what you're talking about.

MILTON: Sure.

STUDENT: You've nailed me before on apology, on really being in the room. So on a recent audition, I went in and the director asked, "What's she reading for?" When the

casting person told him, he said, "Oh, she's too pretty."
Now normally I would just cave in on a comment like
that....

Class laughs.

STUDENT: No! I'm serious! It's a compliment, but not
when I want to get a job, when I'm in there to get a part!
Then it's like the reverse. But I thought about what
you've been teaching me about staying in it, about being
charming. So I said, "Wait a minute. I'm ugly, I'm ugly.
Really!" The director laughed. Then he actually talked to
me for awhile, and said, "Well, you're getting uglier by
the minute." I said, "Let me read for you." And I whipped
around in there and did a real killer audition. And after
I read he said, "You know, I'm not telling you now that
you've got it, and you're not what I had in mind, but I
want you to know that you're good. I'm not saying you got
it now...." I said, "That's okay." Then two weeks later he
called me to tell me I had the part.

Class applauds.

MILTON: Excellent. (*To actor in critique:*) You see? At the
key moment when the director said, "Nah—not right..."
she stayed in it, stayed clever, stayed light and
humorous. And then the talent comes through. The
director starts to open up to her.

ACTOR: Yeah, I think I see....

MILTON: Or like I was saying about Richard Lawson, in
that *Streamers* audition, there wasn't a conversation. No
chit-chat in the office. He just delivered a fucking
concept. I mean, pulling a knife—I wouldn't recommend

it, but he chose to do that and suddenly we were face to face with a concept. He was reading against the best guys in town—I saw a lot of actors for that role, important guys, so-called names. He blew everyone out of the water. So what happened there? What happened to us after his audition?

ACTOR: Well...you...you cast him, I guess.

MILTON: Yeah. And why is that?

ACTOR: Because his concept was so strong, you couldn't do anything else. No one touched what he did.

MILTON: Bingo! Right! You have the power to convince us of how it goes, and then it's yours.

ACTOR: Yeah. I like that.

MILTON: You're a partner in that process, not some "no-name" without influence or power. You are not playing roulette. Your power is the talent you bring, the choices you make, the concept, the point of view. And the more loaded you are, the more vibrant your choice is, the clearer your concept, then the more likely the director will cast you in the part.

ACTOR: That's cool. I like that a lot better. I'll kill it the next time.

MILTON: Excellent. Let's take a break.

An Admin Critique

MILTON: So how's it going for you out there?

ACTRESS: Out where? In the parking lot?

MILTON: In the business, my friend. In the business.

ACTRESS: I know what you meant—I was just trying to avoid the topic.

MILTON: Do you work?

ACTRESS: I think the stock answer here is to say, "Not as much as I want." 98.6% of the actors say that, right?

MILTON: No, no.... You're the first ever to have said that to me.

Laughter from class.

MILTON: What are you doing about it?

ACTRESS: Well, damn. Everything you teach! That's a good answer, right?

MILTON: Only if it's true.

ACTRESS: Shit. Milton, I don't know....

MILTON: You have an agent?

ACTRESS: Yes. She doesn't like me, but yes, I have one.

Class laughs.

ACTRESS: Or at least she doesn't get me out as much as I'd like. That's the stock answer, isn't it?

MILTON: Let me get this straight: You don't work as much as you'd like, and your agent doesn't get you out as much as you want.

ACTRESS: I know, I know.... Do I get points for originality?

MILTON: Absolutely. This is all.... So fresh and new. You're the first. I like you—you're funny, talented, smart. But I want to be serious about this as well, and I don't want to upset you....

ACTRESS: Oh go ahead, upset me! I like it! I do, really! Go ahead, hit me!

More laughter.

MILTON: I left my whip at home. Does your agent know you can do great work like you just did tonight?

ACTRESS: Like this? Absolutely not. No way.

MILTON: She seen you act, other than in her office?

ACTRESS: Well, my reel.

MILTON: So. What do you think I would say about that problem?

ACTRESS: Katselas on agents? Let me see. Rent the fucking theatre. Perform two or three really hot scenes that I nailed in class. Send a car. Send some flowers. Do what I need to do to get her there so she can see me at the top of my game, where I can demonstrate my range and my talent. That's the admin ground plan, right?

MILTON: So, like many of my students, most of them even, you know what I teach but you don't do it.

ACTRESS: You're so good to listen to—but you mean we're actually supposed to do it?

MILTON: Right. Listen, you're sharp. And funny. You're intelligent. And no, you're not alone in this thing about agents. I believe a lot of actors' agents have no clue about their clients, and I believe that is *your problem to solve.* You're the one with the imagination, the talent, the creativity. You're keeping 90% of the paycheck, so you should be doing 90% of the work. Get your agent over here and show them what you're about. Actors are notoriously afraid of talking to their agents. But I believe you must. You have to find a way to get them to understand you, your talent, your casting, the roles for which you believe you should be sent out. Communicate, but keep it simple and professional. As Tom Hanks screamed in that movie: "There's no crying in baseball!" So no crying when talking to your agent. No hostility. No chip. They have a lot of clients. Use some charm. That's part of administration. Let me ask you something else: You go to the movies?

ACTRESS: Sure, I love the movies, I live at the movies, I rent movies—old movies, new movies. Definitely a movie person.

MILTON: But you're not watching like I want you to watch. *(To the class:)* Don't just watch movies to be sucked in by the filmmakers. Don't just go for entertainment and popcorn. Watch like a surgeon, like those young doctors who observe surgery from above the operating room. Find your part. The real part. The actual part that you could really land if you knew the people who could open the door for you to audition. I truly believe there is a part for most of you in just about any movie, and you could go get those parts. And start building a career. If you're smart about it, and proactive. *(To actress:)* Who do you know in this town?

ACTRESS: I know the doorman at that really hot club on Sunset. I forget his name....

MILTON: You are funny. What directors do you know? What directors do you admire, even if you don't know them? What producers? What writers?

ACTRESS: Okay, okay, I admit it! I'm really bad at this. I like the acting part. The administration...it just goes against my grain to sell myself, to do what you teach in this particular area.

A student interrupts.

STUDENT: Milton, can I say something?

MILTON: Sure.

STUDENT: This admin deal is something I totally learned here. I have a DVD right here in my hand of a movie that I have the lead role in. Last year, I was on vacation in North Carolina, and I was eating lunch with my wife in this diner, and I saw two guys poring over a screenplay at the next table, and I could hear they were producing the movie or whatever. So I think of you. I think of your teaching. I'm the last person who will get up from my table to go and say hello to a stranger. But I forced myself. I got up, just walked over there, stood between them, and said, "So, what's my part?" That was my first line. They laughed, they chatted with me a bit. They said, "Well, the only part we have for a guy your age is the lead." I replied, "So what's the problem?" They laughed again. They ended up reading hundreds of people for the lead female role. I was the only guy who read for the male lead. And here's the DVD.

Class applauds.

MILTON: Beautiful. Excellent. This is administration. I believe everyone in here knows someone who can help get them a job. And certainly everyone in here at least *admires* a known professional who works in this business. Write them a letter. I know no one writes letters anymore—it's all e-mail bullshit. A nice letter, perhaps even handwritten, will stand out.

ACTRESS: I'm way too passive. I just hate this administration stuff, Really really *hate it!* You know that sometimes I spend nights and weekends bringing work home from my day job to help them out? I can do it, this administration, this selling, this getting it out there—for *other people.* I really have to learn to do it for myself.

MILTON: You must. You must. Absolutely. And time? Many of you are surfing the web for at least 1-2 hours a day. Let me follow any of you around for a day and I'll show you where you waste 3-4 hours. You own time. Time doesn't push you around. You push it. In *Dreams Into Action,* I say your career takes a "superhuman effort." It's not something for your spare time once a week. This is work. This is administration. It should be part of your life. Put the time into your training, into fixing your attitudes, into your administration. You think Bill Gates was fucking around? He quit Harvard to build software in a garage for whatever it was—20 hours a day. And yet many actors come to town and just kind of go through the motions, both on the acting front and the business front. No good. You getting me?

ACTRESS: Yeah. What is that thing you say sometimes? I'm ready..."to rock and roll...."

MILTON: Beautiful. So what are you doing tomorrow, dahling?

ACTRESS: Well, dahling, I'm getting up an hour earlier than I normally do, I'm going to research the five people responsible for my five favorite TV shows, I'm going to identify five directors whose films I admired in the last year, I'm finding out when the theatre is available, and scheduling an afternoon to do a couple scenes for my agent. That's to begin with. But tonight, I'm going to celebrate—go out and have a great big piece of delicious, luscious chocolate cake.

MILTON: Now that's more like it! Believe me, you're worth it. You're smart. You're beautiful. And funny. A talented actress. And your life and career are worth the effort.

Wake Me, I'm Dreaming....

Frankie and Johnny

ACTRESS: Well, I guess I'll cop to something right off the bat—when you first assigned me to do this scene with him, I was not very happy. Because...I mean, it's weird to say this now, but I just didn't like him. I didn't know him, but I knew I wouldn't like him.

MILTON: I see. You know what that was about?

ACTRESS: Well, just a perception I guess, that he would be difficult to work with. A friend of mine said he was hard to work with, and that didn't help.

MILTON: No. It didn't.

ACTRESS: Straight up commissary talk. I read that chapter. And there I was, right in the middle of it. So I thought to myself, "Look, you've been studying with this guy, he's been talking about your acting and your attitude, why not just actually do what he suggests for once, instead of thinking you know better than him?" So the first thing I did was tell my friend, "Hey, I'm going to do this scene with him, it's an assignment, and I'd like to kill it. So that comment doesn't really help me." And it was easy—she backed off right away and said I was right.

MILTON: Who sent you? St. Peter?

Class laughs.

ACTRESS: So I just decided to go in with an open mind. And actually, he's a nice guy. He takes the acting seriously. And it was totally professional. And we ended up, I think, doing a good scene. I mean, I feel like I connected with him personally, that I was really listening and responding, which is what you've been wanting me to do in my acting.

MILTON: You bet. Excellent. *(To the scene partner:)* Anything from you?

ACTOR: Yeah. I wasn't exactly a fan of hers, either. I thought she was glib, I didn't think she was really interested in doing serious work here. But it was the same thing—you've been on my case about having a chip on my shoulder, about my hostility. And I thought, "Either I quit this joint, or I try to nail this problem, right here."

MILTON: Is it Christmas or something? What's going on?

Laughter.

ACTOR: So first rehearsal: I show up early at the theatre. I set up everything for rehearsal before she even gets here. I noticed she's always drinking Starbucks, so I got her a Starbucks drink, had that ready for her. And then a flower on the desk. Because, you know, I'm not chasing her, I got a girlfriend, but in the scene—it's supposed to be a romantic scene. So. You know.

ACTRESS: I was blown away. First rehearsal, and he's there early with catering. I couldn't believe it. And right away, it was like all that prejudice I had against him just disappeared. It seemed like a real gesture, saying, "Hey, let's work together. I'm looking forward to this." And yeah, it was perfect for the scene.

MILTON: Uh huh. *(Beat.)* I'm waiting to wake up. I know I'm about to wake up.

More laughter.

MILTON: I'm floored. I mean, I talk about attitude. I talk about the right choices, administration. I talk about these things because I believe they will affect the acting, the ability to work with people, the ability to move ahead in this business. And here it is, the whole thing, right in front of us. This girl, just wonderful in the scene, getting past the glibness. That's gone. The guy with a chip no more. Just charm. Right?

CLASS: Yes!

MILTON: To be honest, I wonder sometimes whether I'm being too simplistic with my teaching. "You're hostile. You've got a chip. Knock it off. Smile." I mean, is that really going to change anyone? I guess it can. So here you have the fusion of all three branches of my teaching, nailed simply and easily. They each have acting problems and are assigned to do a scene together. But first they check their attitudes at the door—that's the decision within each of them to work with the other, to give it a real shot. With that attitude, she then does a little administration—that's the choice to tell her friend to knock off the negative gossip so she can work. His administration was to show up early and bring her coffee. They build a little trust, they learn to get along. And then the real payoff: The acting work here is the best either of you have ever done in class. That's the real point of all this. It was connected. Romantic. Real. Emotional. Nothing much for me to say here but "Bravo." Bravo to both of you—you give me some hope that maybe I should keep doing this. I'm going to leave now, before I wake up and realize this was just a dream.

So there you have it for this time around. The most important part of all of this is the craft of acting. That's what means the most to me. The attitude and administration—these are songs to accompany that important journey, and can make for a beautiful, melodic dance. Remember, you are the future. You hold in your hands a tremendous power and creativity. I wish you, always, great success.

Epilogue

When my mother, Dena, was a young girl in the town of Tripoli, in her native Greece, a small group of actors moved next door. She befriended them and often took some food to them. Her mother got angry about this, because the family was poor and didn't have much extra to give. But Dena continued to bring them food, sometimes sneaking out of the house so her mother would not see her helping the actors.

They liked her very much even before she brought them food, but being actors, let's just say the food helped cement the relationship. So they would take her to their rehearsals and then to the performances. This group of actors and my mother became very close.

Years later, in Pittsburgh, I was deciding whether to be an actor or not. My father and uncle objected, because they thought I would become gay! But my mother put her foot down and said, "Let him do what he wants." So I went to university as an actor, and then afterwards on to New York to follow my dream. When I lived in New York, as weird as it sounds, I would on occasion send my laundry back home to Pittsburgh for my mother to do. She would in turn send it back, always with some Greek cookies or cake, wrapped carefully in the package, along with twenty or thirty dollars. So here she was, years later, in another time, a totally different circumstance, 5,000 miles away, once again helping actors....

You could say I became a teacher and director and wrote this book to continue the work my mother started many years ago in Greece.

Acknowledgments

For their dedication and support on the teaching staff at the Beverly Hills Playhouse over the years: Allen Barton, Rob Brownstein, Art Cohan, Gloria Gifford, Gary Grossman, Bill Howey, Gary Imhoff, Terry Jastrow, Jocelyn Jones, Richard Lawson, Al Mancini, Sirri Murad, Rick Podell, Joe Santos, Bill Sorrells, Jeffrey Tambor, Chick Vennera, and Allen Williams.

For a particularly attentive and helpful reading of this manuscript: Fred Barton, Peter Levin and Peter Wexler.

For their friendship, support and work with me: Irene Dirmann, Avraham Inlender, Eric Leonard, and Jim Pickett. And for his guidance: L. Ron Hubbard.

Index

293

MILTON KATSELAS